# NO CONTRACT, NO PEACE

## A Legal Guide to Contract Campaigns, Strikes, and Lockouts

ROBERT M. SCHWARTZ

# NO CONTRACT, NO PEACE

## A Legal Guide to Contract Campaigns, Strikes, and Lockouts

*Drawings by Nick Thorkelson*

work
rights
press

WORK RIGHTS PRESS
CAMBRIDGE, MASSACHUSETTS

*No Contract, No Peace: A Legal Guide to Contract Campaigns, Strikes, and Lockouts*

Copyright © 2014 by Robert M. Schwartz

First edition published 2006 under the title: *Strikes, Picketing and Inside Campaigns*

ISBN 978-0-945902-24-9
Library of Congress Number: 2013920553

Work Rights Press
Box 391066
Cambridge, Massachusetts 02139
800-576-4552
www.workrightspress.com

Printed by union labor in Canada

Other books by Robert M. Schwartz: *The Legal Rights of Union Stewards; How to Win Past Practice Grievances; The FMLA Handbook; Just Cause: A Union Guide to Winning Disciplinary Grievances.* Order form on page 205.

"We have petitioned, we have remonstrated, we have supplicated, we have prostrated ourselves at the foot of the throne, but it has been all in vain. We must fight—I repeat it, sir, we must fight."

*—Patrick Henry, American revolutionary*

"Experienced unions know that the threat of a strike is their most effective bargaining device."

*—Employer's Guide to Strike Planning and Prevention*

"[The strike] is an economic weapon which in great measure implements and supports the principles of the collective bargaining system."

*—NLRB v. Erie Resistor Corp. (U.S. Supreme Court)*

"As we enter our third month of a strike against Vons and Pavilions and a lockout imposed by Ralphs and Albertsons, it is obvious that we are up against a pack of brutal, arrogant, and heartless wolves in the corporate world."

*—UFCW Local 324*

# Contents

# Author's Note

THIS BOOK IS MEANT to help unions win better contracts. Good results can sometimes be obtained through spirited arguments at the bargaining table. But if the employer is intransigent or intent on driving down standards, the union may need to carry out an aggressive on-the-job campaign or a full-fledged strike.

Militant actions require bold leaders and courageous members. Avoiding the many trip-wires in the *National Labor Relations Act (NLRA)* is also a necessity. A union that ignores the law risks discharges, damage suits, injunctions, even decertification.

It was not meant to be this way. In 1935, the U.S. Congress enacted the NLRA to enable workers to engage in collective action without fear of losing their jobs. Section 7 of the Act says that employees have a right to take part in "concerted" activities. Section 8 forbids retaliation. Section 13 declares the right to strike.

In the years since, however, Congress, the courts, and the National Labor Relations Board (NLRB) have created many barriers to strikes. The first blow came in 1938, when the U.S. Supreme Court's *Mackay Radio* decision allowed employers to hire permanent replacements during economic strikes. The *Taft-Hartley Act of 1947* banned unions from picketing "secondary" employers. In 1984, the NLRB imposed strict new standards for picket line conduct.

Restrictive laws, court injunctions, and the increasing ability of employers to move operations have lead some unionists to conclude that labor can no longer win strikes. This is a mistake. As Steve Early's foreword chronicles, many unions have found that a combination of creative inside campaigns, short-term walkouts, and full-fledged strikes can still achieve victories.

Historically the fighting spirit of American trade unions has been unrivaled. No other labor movement has battled employers more frequently or more bravely. *No Contract, No Peace* is for those who want that legacy to continue.

Robert M. Schwartz

January 2014

*The author can be reached at robertmschwartz@comcast.net.*

# Acknowledgments

**M**ANY LABOR ACTIVISTS AND ATTORNEYS offered valuable insights as I worked on this book. I thank them heartily. Unionists include Jeff Bolen (UFCW), David Cohen (UE), Edward Collins (IBEW), Richard de Vries (IBT), Steve Early (CWA), Frank Hallstead (IBT), Paul Hannon (USWA), Peter Knowlton (UE), Tom Leedham (IBT), Dana Simon (MNA), John Murphy (IBT), Richard O'Flaherty (ATU), Ellen Wallace (UAW), and Rand Wilson (SEIU). Attorneys include Ellis Boal, Bryan Decker, Bruce Feldacker, Julius Getman, Polly Halfkenny, Aaron Krakow, Gay Semel, Alan Shapiro, and Christopher Souris.

# Caveats

• *No Contract, No Peace* is based on the *National Labor Relations Act (NLRA)*, a law covering most, but not all, private sector workplaces. Unions in sectors not under the NLRA's jurisdiction— in particular, the airline, railroad, and government sectors—must look elsewhere for guidance.

• Thirteen states—Alaska, California, Colorado, Hawaii, Idaho, Illinois, Louisiana, Minnesota, Montana, Ohio, Oregon, Pennsylvania, and Vermont—permit government workers to strike. In these states, some of the rules described in this book may apply. All other states prohibit strikes by public employees. Strikes by federal government workers, including postal workers, are also illegal.

• The first edition of this book was published in 2006, during the George W. Bush era. Since 2009, members appointed to the National Labor Relations Board (NLRB) by President Barack Obama have issued several significant decisions advancing union rights. These include requiring employers to continue dues checkoff after contract expiration, allowing unions to employ more aggressive tactics against secondaries, and restricting lockouts. Challenges to some of these rulings are still pending in the appeals courts.

• The endnotes to *No Contract, No Peace* cite legal cases, identify exceptions to general rules, and provide supplemental information. Readers should not ignore them.

# Foreword
## By Steve Early

I N THE SUMMER OF 2011 labor unrest from coast to coast provided a sharp rebuttal to the widely held view that the strike is
dead and buried in America. Even as veterans of the Professional
Air Traffic Controllers Organization (PATCO) gathered to com-
memorate the 30th anniversary of their historic struggle, a new gen-
eration of strikers was taking on big national employers like Verizon
and Kaiser Permanente.

For two weeks in August of 2011, 45,000 Verizon workers
walked-out from Massachusetts to Virginia in a high-profile strike
against contract concessions. A month later 20,000 nurses and other
union members joined them opposing pension and health care give-
backs at Kaiser Permanente in California.

These same hospital workers staged another California-wide work stoppage in early 2012. Later that year, 26,000 public school teachers hit the bricks successfully in Chicago. In cities round the country, Wal-Mart employees and fast food workers followed them, protesting low pay and unfair labor practices in their nonunion workplaces.

## Hard times for labor

PATCO's destruction in 1981 ushered in three decades of difficult strikes and lockouts for all kinds of workers, invariably triggered by management demands for takeaways. With renewed momentum from the recession of 2008, this employer drive for contract concessions continues unabated today—in both private and public sectors.

Even in the 1980s, some strike activity—NYNEX and Pittston Coal, for example—resulted in union victories. But far more anti-concessions battles ended badly at companies like Phelps-Dodge, Greyhound, Hormel, Continental Airlines, and International Paper. That grim trend continued in the 1990s with setbacks at Caterpillar, Bridgestone/Firestone, A.E. Staley, and the Detroit News and Free Press.

Striking became a high stakes venture involving considerable legal, financial, and organizational risks. As a result, fewer unions dared to fight back in traditional fashion and the pool of union members and leaders with direct strike experience has shrunk steadily. Fewer unions now grapple with the challenge of maintaining strike capacity through measures like raising dues to finance bigger strike funds that pay out guaranteed weekly benefits. Instead, many focus primarily on organizing and political action as the way to rebuild union clout.

As Robert Schwartz argues in this invaluable book, contract campaigns and strikes remain essential parts of any strategy to revitalize the labor movement, defend past bargaining gains, and make new contract breakthroughs. Using educational tools like *No Contract, No Peace*, union members need to analyze labor's past victories and defeats so the lessons of these battles become the basis for future success, not a recurring pattern of organizational failure.

## General strikes

Union strength and workers' strike effectiveness have long been connected. Throughout history, work stoppages have altered the balance of power between labor and capital in single workplaces and across entire industries. Strikes have won shorter hours and safer conditions, fostered new forms of worker organization, and acted as incubators for class-consciousness, rank-and-file leadership, and political activism. In some countries, strikes have challenged and changed dictatorial governments, like those that fell in the Middle East during the Arab Spring of 2011.

General strikes are still used in Western Europe for mass mobilization and political protest. In recent years, millions of workers in France, Italy, Spain, and Greece have struck against pension cuts, labor law changes, and other "austerity" measures proposed by their own national governments. In November of 2012, they engaged in coordinated cross-border strike activity throughout the European Union.

In 2006, hundreds of thousands of foreign-born workers and their allies participated in similar—but more rare—political strike activity in America. Their "rallying for immigrant rights" took the form of successive one-day protests culminating in a massive work stay-away on May 1, 2006. Union members and even more nonunion workers took to the streets, along with family members and community supporters, to block anti-immigrant legislation. An estimated 3.7 to 5 million people joined the escalating protests. As reported by the *New York Times*:

> Lettuce, tomatoes and grapes went unpicked in fields in California and Arizona, which contribute more than half the nation's produce, as scores of growers let workers take the day off. Truckers who move 70 percent of the goods in ports in Los Angeles and Long Beach, Calif did not work. Meatpacking companies, including Tyson Foods and Cargill, closed plants in the Midwest and the West employing more than 20,000 people, while the flower and produce markets in downtown Los Angeles stood largely and eerily empty.

## Pushing the envelope

One big obstacle to general strike activity in the U.S. is the legal straitjacket imposed by the *National Labor Relations Act (NLRA)*. The most effective strike tactics and forms of workplace solidarity are effectively outlawed. Successful union contract campaigners must push the envelope with creative, militant, and direct action tactics.

Sometimes that means staying on the job and letting the contract expire—an option well explained by Schwartz in Chapter 2, "Working Without a Contract." Confronted by strike contingency planning by management that would blunt the impact of any walkout, workers may need to depart from their union tradition of "no contract, no work," while applying pressure on the employer in other ways.

Over the last 25 years, telephone workers in the northeast have repeatedly walked out or worked without a contract, depending on the circumstances at the time. In 1989, 60,000 members of the Communications Workers of America (CWA) and the International Brotherhood of Electrical Workers (IBEW) waged a high-impact strike over medical cuts threatened at the phone company then known as NYNEX. The workers used ambulatory picketing tactics like those recommended in *No Contract, No Peace* and targeted top company officials and their allies in places where they least expected it. (See Chapter 6, "Making it Personal.")

In the Appalachian coalfields that same year, the United Mine Workers (UMW) made their 12-month walkout against Pittston a national labor cause after working without a contract for months. The union mobilized sympathy strikes at other companies, linked arms with Rev. Jesse Jackson, used civil disobedience tactics, staged the first plant occupation since the 1930s, and created "Camp Solidarity" to host strike supporters from around the country. Even an avalanche of injunctions, fines, and damage suits did not deter miners and their families.

Just a few years later, West Virginia aluminum workers, locked out by Ravenswood, applied many crucial lessons of the Pittston struggle in a wide-ranging corporate campaign orchestrated by the United Steel Workers of America (USWA). The USWA leveraged its extensive international labor connections to put pressure on key financial institutions and investors tied to the employer. (See Chapter 5, "Striking Allied Enterprises") Despite massive hiring of replacement workers and other union-busting measures, Ravenswood was finally forced to end its lockout and settle with the USWA.

On the west coast, ILWU dockworkers and members of UNITE-HERE used mass action tactics to turn the table on offensive lockouts by management. In the case of UNITE-HERE, coordinated struggles by hotel workers in different cities resulted in some chains agreeing to common contract expiration dates, thus boosting union bargaining clout in the future. In July 2013, a four-year corporate campaign and global boycott resulted in a favorable settlement for 5,000 hotel employees of the Hyatt Hotels Corp.— and an organizing rights agreement with Hyatt that will facilitate future UNITE-HERE organizing.

## Framing the issues

The traditional open-ended contract strike made its strongest comeback in 1997 with a nationwide walkout by 190,000 United Parcel Service (UPS) workers, the largest strike since 1983. Other unions have long appreciated picket line observance by Teamster drivers. This time the rest of labor returned the favor with a tremendous outpouring of support for the striking drivers and package handlers.

The way the Teamsters framed their dispute with UPS helped generate an unusual degree of public sympathy. The main strike objective was to create more full-time jobs, by thwarting the company's strategy of expanding its already huge part-time workforce. "Part-time America doesn't work," the strikers proclaimed, successfully investing their contract fight with larger social meaning. The UPS walkout not only defeated givebacks, it led to many gains in full-time job creation. The strike became a rallying point for everyone concerned about the spread of contingent labor and the accompanying erosion of job security and benefit coverage throughout the U.S. economy.

## Defending retirement and healthcare rights

The biggest negotiating challenge facing labor in recent years has been maintaining affordable medical care and defined benefit pensions. To keep public opinion on their side, unions must find ways to make these fights a defense of retirement security and better health care coverage for everyone.

In 2003, for example, 18,000 General Electric workers staged a two-day national walkout to protest medical plan changes at their company, but the strike demand stressed by many UE and IUE-CWA locals was "Health Care for all, not health cuts at GE!" Through joint rallies, picketing and sticker-wearing, union and community activists emphasized the common bond between workers with and without job-based insurance. Both need real health care reform that would make medical coverage universal, publicly funded, and no longer controlled by employers.

## The lockout trend

Recently more employers have been landing the first blow in major contract disputes. In 2011 there were 17 lockouts in the United States, a record 90 per cent of all major work stoppages (those affecting 1,000 workers or more). Among those locked out were professional basketball and football players, USWA members at Cooper Tire in Ohio, Teamsters at Sotheby's in New York, and American Crystal Sugar workers in Minnesota, Iowa, and North Dakota. Even in more labor-friendly Canada, Caterpillar used the lockout tactic to defeat the Canadian Auto Workers.

When management sends workers home, unions must be prepared with countermeasures of their own. Chapter 15 provides important advice on dealing with lockouts, like the 10-month Teamster campaign for a fair contract at Sotheby's, the famous Manhattan art dealer. To win that fight, workers joined forces with Occupy Wall Street to stage a series of colorful and disruptive protests directed at the "One Percenters" who patronize and profit from Sotheby's.

## Generating public support

On a far larger scale, the Chicago Teachers Union (CTU) showdown with Democratic Mayor Rahm Emanuel in September 2012 showed the importance of seeking broad public support. After restructuring internally to rebuild its workplace steward network, the CTU carefully prepared for its 7-day strike with systematic outreach to parents, churches, and community organizations. Strong ties to the community enabled the union to neutralize much of the anti-union sentiment that city hall, the school board, the Chicago media, and corporate-backed "education reform" groups tried to whip up. Instead of allowing themselves to be depicted as greedy and selfish, the teachers positioned themselves as defenders of quality education for low-income Chicagoans.

The high-profile strikes among food service, retail, and warehouse workers in 2012-13 demonstrate that labor militancy can take many different forms and still have a positive impact, even without union recognition or formal bargaining. The key to success—whether you're on strike for a day, locked out for weeks, or pursuing non-strike strategies—is creativity, careful planning, and rank-and-file involvement.

*No Contract, No Peace* lays out the full range of options available to union members. This guide should be used in every labor education program, particularly training sessions for bargaining committee members and contract campaign organizers. Front-line union nego-tiators will invariably face difficult decisions about how to fight back with the greatest workplace impact and the least risk or cost to the rank-and-file. *No Contract, No Peace* can help union leaders at every level make well-informed decisions that lead to victory, not defeat.

Steve Early, former International Representative for the Communica-tions Workers of America (CWA), was involved in contract negotiations and strike activity by telecom and manufacturing workers for three decades. His books include *Save Our Unions: Dispatches from a Movement in Distress* (Monthly Review Press, 2013).

# 1
# Mounting a Dynamic Contract Campaign

*Mobilizing the membership* ◆ *A thousand cuts*

IN YEARS PAST unions could often win better contracts by submitting reasonable proposals and making compelling arguments. With both sides seeking common ground, deals eventually emerged. This has changed. In today's dysfunctional economic climate, straightforward bargaining frequently comes up empty. Employers come to the table with lengthy lists of takeaways and refuse to compromise. Claiming impasse at the earliest opportunity, they threaten to carry out their final offer or impose a lockout. To cope with these realities many unions are turning to militant contract campaigns. Creative and aggressive tactics can demonstrate the solidarity and resolve of union members and their willingness to act.

## Mobilizing the membership

Successful contract campaigns rely on widespread member participation. Months before negotiations begin, the union selects a contract action team. Using individual and group meetings, surveys, and house calls, the team reaches out to every worker, soliciting suggestions for bargaining demands and ideas for exerting pressure. Films, speakers, and handouts educate members about labor struggles.

Rank and filers are often asked to join the union negotiating team. The entire membership can be encouraged to attend bargaining sessions.[1] Meetings, handbills, newsletters, e-mails, direct mail, and internet postings keep everyone informed.

The union can reject bargaining ground rules that limit member involvement—for example, a rule that negotiations be kept secret. Because ground rules are not "mandatory" subjects of bargaining, an employer cannot make a particular procedure a condition for taking part in negotiations.[2]

As bargaining proceeds, the union engages in a variety of pressure tactics such as buttons, shirts, solidarity days, rallies, and marches. Informational picketing may be conducted before and after shifts. Work-to-rule and boycott campaigns may also be instituted. Every member should be encouraged to participate.

Vigorous contract campaigns often trigger employer unfair labor practices—violations of the *National Labor Relations Act (NLRA)*. Examples include restrictions, threats, retaliation, and surveillance. Such actions can backfire by giving the union a legal basis for calling an unfair labor practice strike (see Chapter 13). Think of a football lineman who jumps forward in the hope of drawing the other team offside.

Another union strategy to pressure the employer is to let the contract expire and stay on the job. Contract expiration cancels the no-strike clause. With the union able to walk out at any moment, a cloud of uncertainty will envelope the employer and its customers. Expiration also extinguishes the contract's "management rights" and "zipper" clauses. This ends the employer's ability to make unilateral changes in assignments, workloads, hours, and other day-to-day matters. Instead, it will have to give the union advance notice and bargain to impasse before taking action. If the employer carries on as before, the union will be able to file a stream of unfair-labor-practice charges—forcing the employer to delay decisions and incur legal expenses.

The employer may respond to an aggressive contract campaign by locking out the bargaining unit. This too can backfire. As explained in Chapter 15, from a union perspective a lockout has several advantages over a strike. The employer will not be able to hire permanent replacements, unemployment insurance benefits are likely to be awarded, and, in certain circumstances, workers can win back pay.

## A thousand cuts

Job actions—a "thousand cuts" —are the heart of a contract campaign. As one organizer put it:

> The key is that you create a situation so that management, from the time they get up in the morning till the time they go to bed, they worry about what you're doing. And if you're doing a good job, they wake up with nightmares.

A 2009 campaign by CWA Local 1298 is a good example. The campaign featured rallies, stickers, television ads, T-shirts with messages at football games and American Idol tryouts, red shirts on Tuesdays and Thursdays, red and black balloons at work, bags of nuts with signs saying "AT&T is Offering Us Peanuts," bubble gum with fliers reading "AT&T Proposals Blow," and "Shake, Rattle and Roll" days where employees put pennies in empty bottles, stood at their desks, and shook the bottles.

Contract campaign activities can help lay the groundwork for a strike by training workers in active techniques, establishing communications networks, and publicizing the dispute to local media, clergy, and the community.

**Buttons, stickers and shirts.** Workers have a well-established legal right to express their opinions on buttons, shirts, hats, and armbands while on the job.[3] Typical legends: "No contract, no peace," "Fight for a fair contract," "No give-backs," "Stop union busting." A solidarity day—everyone wearing black, red, or union T-shirts—is protected by the NLRA unless it conflicts with an enforced dress code. One NLRB case required a company to tolerate clothing resembling prison garb.[4] Another approved a button reading: "Shut management down or 100,000 Teamsters will."[5]

An employer can bar insignia that is obscene, provokes violence, disparages products, affects concentration, or harms relations with customers.[6] Speculation is not enough: the employer must have tangible evidence that the insignia is having or will have the claimed effect.[7]

In some "special circumstances," an employer can ban all forms of insignia. The NLRB has recognized this exception in direct patient care areas[8] and when a consistently enforced business plan mandates a particular public image, such as a neatly uniformed delivery driver.[9]

Even in such circumstances, a ban on union insignia is illegal if the employer discriminates. For example, a delivery company cannot order a uniformed driver to remove a "Contract now!" button if it previously allowed political, religious, or social-cause insignia.[10] Nor may an employer enforce a rule that is overly broad. For example, a hospital may not issue a rule banning insignia throughout the institution.[11]

Ordering an employee to remove protected union insignia is an unfair labor practice.[12] Issuing discipline because an employee wears such insignia or refuses an instruction to remove it is also illegal.[13]

**Handbills.** Under NLRA rules, employees must be permitted to distribute union literature to other employees or the public in non-working areas during nonworking time, unless the employer can demonstrate that prohibiting such activity is necessary to maintain productivity or to avoid undue disruption.[14] Nonworking time includes before and after work and breaks. Nonworking areas generally include parking lots, front steps, break rooms, and cafeterias. Company policies that forbid lawful handbilling or require prior permission are unlawful.[15] Union flyers can express outrage and urge employees to stand together. Management may not order employees to stop, impose penalties, or call the police.[16] Nor may it film the activity or record names.[17]

Employees may place flyers on tables in cafeterias or break rooms and on automobile windshields in the company parking lot.[18] Management may not remove the materials.

Absent special circumstances, off-duty employees must be permitted to hand out flyers to customers, clients, and the general public while on nonwork areas of the employers premises such as driveways and entrances.[19] Flyers can ask patrons to tell the employer to bargain a fair contract. They can also ask patrons to take their business elsewhere.[20] Management may not retaliate in any way.

**Rallies.** Daily or weekly mass rallies are standard fare in contract campaigns. [21] Although the usual location is a public street or sidewalk, employees have a right to peacefully assemble on outside areas of the employer's premises, such as parking lots or walkways.[22] As long as rallies do not disrupt operations, or traffic, management cannot film or write down names.[23]

**Informational picketing.** Informational picketing (picketing not part of a strike) adds force to a contract campaign. The NLRA protects the activity unless the contract has a no-picketing clause.[24] Typical signs: "Fighting for a fair contract," "Honk if you're with us." Bullhorns, drums, and banners can enliven the activity. Family members can join. In the absence of violence or blocking, the employer may not film or take photographs.[25]

**Work-to-rule.** In a "work-to-rule" action, employees scrupulously follow company policies, procedures, and standards, especially directives dealing with safety and hygiene. No one  volunteers for extra duties, performs off the clock, or works at more than normal speed. Everyone takes full breaks.

The NLRB has not drawn a clear line between protected work-to-rule activity and an unprotected slowdown or "partial strike." One decision, however, prohibited discipline against employees who deliberately left their personal tools at home. In language suggesting a wide application, the Board declared:

> Where an action is voluntary, the concerted refusal by employees to perform that action is a protected concerted activity and does not constitute an unlawful partial strike.[26]

Workers should be instructed to carry the campaign out unobtrusively, without open defiance. Direct orders from supervisors to perform tasks should be obeyed.

**Boycott.** Unions have a right to seek support from customers and the public. This includes a plea to boycott the employer's products.[27]

Boycott activities can include:

- Handbills to persons approaching the facility
- Handbills at trade shows
- Signs on automobiles
- Airplane banners
- Bridge banners
- Letters to customers, places of worship, and civic groups

**Stockholders and directors.** Campaigns can be directed against officers, stockholders, trustees, and directors. The union can send letters, make visits, distribute flyers, and picket homes.

Because the NLRA prohibits secondary picketing (see pages 55–56), the union usually cannot picket a business owned or managed by a stockholder or a director. It can, however, use flyers and large stationary banners to ask patrons to take their business elsewhere (see Chapter 9).

# Questions and Answers

**Personnel policy**

Q. A rule in our personnel handbook prohibits employees from remaining on the property after work. Can it be enforced against a union rally in the company parking lot?

A. No. A policy that effectively prohibits lawful concerted activity violates the NLRA—even if it was enacted for a legitimate reason.[28] Employees may not be disciplined for violating an illegal rule.[29] Nor may the employer charge an employee with insubordination for ignoring an order to comply.[30]

### Overtime moratorium

Q. Our contract says employees can decline overtime requests. To give our bargaining team some heft, can we tell everyone to refuse ?

A. Not safely. Section 8(d)(4) of the NLRA prohibits a union from striking for a new contract from the day the union requests negotiations to the day the contract expires. Refusing overtime as a group is considered a strike.[31]

### Uniform picketing

Q. Can management bar us from wearing our uniforms during informational picketing?

A. No, unless a company rule prohibits employees from wearing uniforms off duty and the rule has been consistently enforced.[32]

### Refusal to bargain

Q. Can management refuse to bargain until the union stops picketing, holding rallies, and carrying out other contract campaign tactics?

A. No. An employer's bargaining duty does not disappear because the union engages in concerted activities.[33]

### Social media

Q. Our personnel policy says "Employees may not use the internet to make disparaging, discriminatory, or defamatory comments about the company or the employee's superiors." Can the company apply this rule to employees who attack the company on Facebook?

A. No. Posting contract or other union-related messages on the internet is protected by the NLRA.[34]

### Customer relations

Q. The union president told management that unless more progress was made in negotiations she would notify customers to expect a strike. The HR director responded that the company would sue her for "tortious interference." Is the president at risk?

A. No. Unions can contact customers to seek support, urge a boycott, or warn of a possible strike.[35] A threat to sue an employee or a union for taking part in protected activity is an unfair labor practice.[36]

### Honest mistake

Q. We made a mistake in one of our leaflets describing the company's bargaining position. Can we be disciplined for spreading falsehoods?

A. No. An employee cannot be punished for distributing inaccurate literature unless the inaccuracy is deliberate or malicious.[37]

### Charity event

Q. The President of the company is receiving a charity award at a local restaurant. What can we do at the event?

A. You can leaflet and hold stationary banners attacking the President and the company and ask persons not to go in. But you cannot picket the restaurant or disrupt the meal.

# 2

# Working Without a Contract

*What's at risk?* ◆ *Playing a new hand*

**W**HEN A COLLECTIVE BARGAINING AGREEMENT is on the verge of expiring without a promising replacement on the near horizon, the union has three basic options: temporarily extend the existing agreement, strike, or work without a contract. Under each approach, the employer must continue to bargain over a new agreement. In past years unions almost always either extended their contracts or called a strike. Working without a contract was regarded as hazardous, enabling the employer to eliminate long-standing benefits including dues checkoff. In recent times the law has improved and unions have recognized that working without a contract can give them valuable cards to play.

Released from the contract's no-strike restrictions, a union that works without a contract can call "warning" or "grievance" walkouts. Moreover, free of the management-rights clause, the union can force the employer to engage in extensive bargaining over job assignments, schedules, workloads, and other day-to-day matters. Perhaps most importantly, the employer and its customers will face a tense period of uncertainty about whether and when the union will unleash a punishing contract strike.

## What's at risk?

It is sometimes believed that once a contract expires, an employer can immediately reduce wages and benefits and repudiate past practices. This is a misconception. With three exceptions (see below), the *National Labor Relations Act (NLRA)* requires employers to maintain the status quo, including wage rates, benefits, and past practices.[38]

The only areas in which an employer can take unilateral action following contract expiration are: union security, arbitration procedures, and "permissive" subjects of bargaining. In all other matters, the employer must give notice to the union and bargain to a good faith impasse.

**Union security.** When a collective bargaining agreement expires, provisions requiring employees to join the union and remain in good standing are no longer binding.[39] This allows the employer to retain workers who refuse to join the union or pay dues. A different rule applies to voluntary dues checkoff. According to a landmark 2012 Board decision, an employer must adhere to dues checkoff practices following contract expiration just as it must observe existing wage rates and other conditions of employment.[40]

**Arbitration.** An employer can refuse to arbitrate almost all grievances that are filed after the contract expires. An exception is a grievance over rights that accrued while the contract was in effect. Although newly-filed grievances may not be arbitrable, the employer must meet with the union and provide relevant information.[41]

The loss of compulsory arbitration will weaken the union's ability to challenge discharges and other discipline. However, if an employee is disciplined because of union or contract campaign activities, the union can file a discrimination charge at the NLRB.

**Permissive subjects.** Contract expiration permits an employer to revoke agreements and practices that relate to "permissive" subjects of bargaining.[42] Matters of concern include pensions and medical benefits for workers who are already retired. See page 47 for a list of other permissive subjects.

**Matters bargained to impasse.** With the contract no longer in force, the employer may be able to implement some or all of its bargaining proposals, including proposals to reduce wages and benefits. This sounds ominous, but several limitations apply:

- An employer may not implement a bargaining proposal unless the parties are at impasse on the contract as a whole. Deadlock on one proposal ordinarily does not permit the employer to declare impasse.[43] A negative ratification vote does not create impasse if the union is willing to adjust its position.

- The employer cannot declare impasse on a final offer if a request for information on an important issue is pending, if the offer includes a permissive subject of bargaining to which the union has objected, or if the employer committed a ULP that adversely affected negotiations.

- The employer may not make a change that significantly varies from its final offer. For example, if an employer that is seeking a 5% cut in starting wages reaches impasse on the contract, it cannot make a 10% cut. If a health insurance proposal includes decreases and increases, the employer cannot carry out the decreases without the increases.

- Even if impasse exists on the contract as a whole, the employer may not implement the following proposals: a ban on strikes or other concerted activities, a management-rights provision that allows the employer to change conditions of work without bargaining, or a new grievance and arbitration procedure.[44]

**Pointer:** To forestall impasse:
- Make counterproposals to all employer demands.
- Submit detailed information requests.[45]
- Never admit that negotiations are deadlocked — not even to members.
- Never use the terms "final" or "deal-breaker."
- Never characterize a demand as "nonnegotiable."
- Always assert a willingness to compromise.

- Never ask or encourage the employer to make a final offer.
- Put off mediation until the employer is about to declare impasse.
- Never leave a meeting without attempting to schedule another.
- Make at least a minor change on a key issue.

## Playing a new hand

A union that allows its contract to expire can engage in several tactics unavailable when the contract was in force.

**Warning strike.** Expiration removes any contractual or statutory restrictions on strikes and picketing.[46] This allows the union to call a short-term "warning" or "grievance" strike. It can initiate the walkout at the start, middle, or end of a shift. The strike can include some or all of the bargaining unit. Other than in the health care industry, where the NLRA requires 10-days advance written notice, and in unusually vulnerable workplaces such as prisons, it is not necessary to alert the employer in advance.

> **Pointer:** Do not strike over a grievance that arose while the contract was in effect. The no-strike clause may continue to be in effect over the matter.[47]

Workers who participate in short-term walkouts are protected against retaliation.[48] If the employer is aware of the strike, it cannot count absences as unexcused.[49] Nor can it discipline employees for failing to call in.[50]

> **Pointer:** An employee who is asked why she was absent should say she was on strike or taking part in a union protest. Silence or another explanation may enable the employer to count the absence against her.

*Intermittent strikes.* An NLRA rule makes it difficult for unions to carry out multiple short-term walkouts. The rule denies legal protection to workers who take part in "intermittent strikes."[51] The purpose is to prevent "hit and run" walkouts.

The NLRB defines an intermittent strike as a series of walkouts for a common goal,[52] but it has not definitively stated what makes up a series. In some circumstances, the Board has required three stoppages. For example, a 1975 case declared:

> While there is no magic number as to how many work stoppages must be reached before we can say that they are of a recurring nature, certainly the two work stoppages in the case at bar, which involved a total of 2 days absence from work, do not, in our opinion, evidence the type of pattern of recurring stoppages which would deprive the employees of their Section 7 rights.[53]

In other circumstances the Board has classified two walkouts as an intermittent strike. In one case, the union struck twice within 19 days for a new contract.[54] In another, the union simultaneously engaged in other inside game activities.[55]

**Note:** A short-term strike followed days or weeks later by a full-fledged strike is not an intermittent strike.[56]

To reduce the possibility that the NLRB will classify two walkouts as an intermittent strike, the union should:

- Hold the walkouts for differently stated reasons.
- Hold the walkouts weeks or months apart.
- Hold the walkouts quickly after a triggering event.
- Avoid any reference to a "grievance strike strategy."

*Protecting employees against replacement.* During the course of an economic strike, whether short- or long-term, the employer can hire replacement workers on a permanent basis. When the strike is over, replaced strikers must wait for openings on a preferential recall list (see pages 147–148).

Two tactics can protect strikers against permanent replacement. Soon after the strike begins, the union notifies the employer that strikers will return to work "without conditions" at a particular day and time in the near future. An employer may not hire permanent replacements after it receives such a notice.[57]

---

### RETURN-TO-WORK OFFER

**Date:** Tuesday, February 2, 2014
**Time:** 7:01 a.m.
**To:** Leo Nelson, Production Manager
**From:** Ken Myers, President, Local 21
**Re:** Return-to-work offer

Local 21 hereby notifies the company that at 7:00 a.m. today, Tuesday, February 2, 2014, members of the bargaining unit represented by Local 21 commenced a 24-hour strike for a fair contract. Peaceful picketing will occur at the company's premises.

Strike activity will cease as of 6:59 a.m. February 3, 2013, and an offer to return to work without conditions at 7:00 a.m. on February 3, 2014 is hereby made for all persons in the above-described bargaining unit and all employees who honor the union picket line.

---

The second tactic is to position the walkout as an unfair labor practice (ULP) strike. As explained in Chapter 13, a ULP strike protests an employer violation of the *National Labor Relations Act (NLRA)*. Examples of NLRA violations include threats, unlawful surveillance, refusals to provide information, and unilateral changes.

An employer may not hire permanent replacements for employees who take part in a ULP strike. If new workers are brought in, the employer must terminate them to make room for returning strikers.

**Bargaining on day-to-day decisions.** As mentioned in Chapter 1, when a union contract expires, management rights and zipper clauses in the agreement are no longer in force.[58] This prevents the employer from making any substantial changes in terms and conditions of employment in the absence of notice to the union, an opportunity to bargain, and an overall impasse on bargaining for the new agreement. Changes subject to this rule include disciplinary policies, work rules, job assignments, layoffs, subcontracting, methods of supervision, and workloads.[59] By demanding bargaining and filing ULP charges, the union can force the employer to roll back many day-to-day decisions. Employer violations can create a basis for the union to call a ULP strike.

# Questions and Answers

### Past practice

Q. Before our contract expired, the employer allowed union business agents to enter the workplace whenever they wished to speak with a member. Now, labor relations says the union must give 24 hours advance written notice. Is the new policy lawful?

A. No. Union access to the workplace is a mandatory bargaining subject. The employer cannot make a material change in a past practice without giving prior notice to the union and, if requested, bargaining to agreement or impasse.[60]

### Pay increases

Q. Our contract mandates a 2% wage increase on employee anniversary dates. If we let the contract expire, will the company have to continue this policy?

A. Yes. The duty to continue existing terms includes pay raises in the contract's final year.[61]

### Partial strike

Q. Can a faculty union dramatize a contract campaign by refusing to hand in student grades?

A. Not safely. The NLRA does not protect employees who deliberately fail to complete their assignments, even when the refusal is part of a union protest.[62]

### Sit-in

Q. We are thinking of calling a one-hour strike. Can we stay at our machines?

A. Not safely. Although the NLRB occasionally protects in-plant stoppages,[63] the wisest course is to leave the premises.

### Arbitration

Q. Three grievances are scheduled for arbitration this month. If we let our contract expire, will these cases die?

A. No. The employer must arbitrate grievances filed while the contract was in effect.

### Sickout

**Q.** Our contract has expired. Can we call a sickout to protest company demands?

**A.** Only with care. A sickout is a lawful form of concerted activity if the employer knows or has reason to know that employees are absent due to a union protest.[64] Some unions instruct workers to claim a "mental health day."

### Temp agency contract

**Q.** We struck for two days to oppose the employer's contract offer. The general manager says we will have to wait three days before coming back because he signed a five-day contract with a temporary help contractor. Can we be held out?

**A.** Perhaps. An employer can delay strikers from returning to work if it has a "legitimate and substantial business justification."[65] A replacement contract that extends beyond the end of a strike can serve as a justification if the contractor demanded the engagement period and there was no other way to obtain replacements.[66]

> **Pointer:** Ask for a copy of the contract with the staffing agency and all related documents including correspondence, notes, and emails.

### Lockout

**Q.** Can an employer lock out a union because it conducts a one-day strike?

**A.** This depends. An employer can declare a lockout if it has a legitimate concern that work stoppages will continue and if its operations are highly vulnerable to interruptions.[67] If such fears are unfounded, the lockout may be ruled unlawful.[68]

# 3

# Hitting the Bricks

*Notice requirements ◆ Withdrawing demands on non-mandatory subjects ◆ Pickets ◆ Signs ◆ Conduct ◆ Shared worksite ◆ Targeting outside businesses ◆ Employer ULPs ◆ Injunctions ◆ Corporate campaign*

**A** STRIKE IS A WATERSHED EVENT for a union, its members, and their families. A successful strike can win a better contract and build lasting solidarity. Future negotiations will be easier because the union has shown the capacity to act. As the saying goes: "A good strike lasts forever." If a strike goes badly, however, benefits may be slashed, jobs may be lost, and the union may have to face a decertification vote. Risk-reducing strategies include positioning the walkout as an unfair labor practice strike (Chapter 13), making a pre-emptive return-to-work offer (Chapter 14), and provoking the employer into declaring a lockout (Chapter 15).

An effective strike requires extensive preparation. Well before the contract expires, the union should review picket locations, legal back-up, communication methods, strike pay, unemployment insurance, COBRA, and Medicaid. Secondary targets should be identified, such as branches, subsidiaries, customers, suppliers, and businesses owned by directors. A strike fund should be created and funded.

Most unions put strike votes before the members. Discussions should be candid, going over both the benefits to be gained and the possibility of failure. Members should be aware that the walkout may be lengthy and that the employer may hire permanent replace-ments. Some unions insist that a strike vote garner 90 percent approval.

## Notice requirements

Before hitting the bricks, the union must assure itself that it has served the notices required by Sections 8(d) and (g) of the *National Labor Relations Act (NLRA)*. Otherwise, the strike will be illegal and participants may be discharged.

**Employer notice.** Section 8(d)(1) of the NLRA requires the union to give written notice to the employer that it wants to negotiate a new collective bargaining agreement. The notice must be served on the employer at least 60 days before the expiration of the current agreement (90 days in the health care industry). The union can compose its own notice (see below) or use Form F-7 from the Federal Mediation and Conciliation Service (FMCS). The notice may be mailed, e-mailed, faxed, or hand delivered.

---

**NOTICE TO EMPLOYER**

UTW Local 100 hereby gives notice to Rich Foods that it wishes to terminate the current collective bargaining agreement and negotiate a new agreement.

---

**Mediation agencies.** Section 8(d)(3) of the NLRA requires the union to notify the Federal Mediation and Conciliation Service and the corresponding state labor mediation service that a labor dispute is in progress.[69] These notices must be provided within 30 days of the employer notice (60 days in the health care industry). F7 forms can be used. Most unions send simultaneous notices to the employer and the mediation services. If using U.S. mail, return receipts should be requested.

**Overcoming late notice.** A union that fails to serve a timely employer notice may not strike over a contract unless it serves notice and waits 60 days. If it misses the deadline for serving a mediation agency, it must serve notice and wait 30 days.[70]

**Example:** Local 3 served its employer with a renegotiation notice 60 days before expiration and sent a copy to the FMCS. Negotiations were unsuccessful and the union prepared to strike. The day before expiration, the union realized that it had failed to notify the state labor mediation agency. Instead of conducting an unprotected strike, it served the agency, waited 30 days, and then hit the bricks.

**Note:** The notices specified in Section 8(d) are not necessary for a strike that is called to protest a serious unfair labor practice.[71]

**Health care.** Section 8(g) of the NLRA applies to unions that represent employees of health care institutions, such as hospitals and nursing homes. Such unions must give the institution and the FMCS at least ten days advance written notice of the date and time of a projected strike.[72] The notice should make clear that the union plans to strike *and* picket. It is not necessary to notify a state mediation agency.

**Timing.** A union that gives the notices required by Sections 8(d) and (g) can strike anytime after contact expiration, including the middle of a shift or the start of an important project. Negotiations do not have to be at impasse.

**Note:** In the (rare) circumstance that a striker's absence is likely to cause imminent injury to the employer's property, employees, or clients, the union or the striker must give sufficient advance notice to the employer so that it can make arrangements to avoid damage.[73] The possibility that a walkout will cause spoilage, a drop in sales, or other economic losses does not trigger a duty to give advance notice.[74]

## Withdrawing demands on non-mandatory subjects

The NLRA classifies bargaining subjects as mandatory, permissive, and illegal.[75] Although a union can propose language on a permissive or illegal subject, even repeatedly, a strike over the matter is not protected and participants can be discharged.[76] Before hitting the bricks, the union should review its list of bargaining demands and remove any that involve permissive or illegal subjects. Examples include demands that the employer:

- Expand or change the scope or composition of the bargaining unit.
- Increase pension or health insurance benefits for workers who have already retired.
- Sign a "hot cargo" agreement.
- Withdraw a lawsuit or unfair labor practice charge.
- Agree to interest arbitration.
- Agree not to close a facility.
- Give the union a seat on the board of directors.
- Sign a "neutrality clause" promising not to campaign against union efforts to organize new bargaining units.

**Note:** The union should also remove demands to resolve grievances that arose while the existing or recently expired collective bargaining agreement was in effect.[77]

## Pickets

Picketing publicizes a dispute, discourages persons from entering, and makes it difficult for the employer to operate. A striking union can picket all of the employer's locations, whether or not bargaining unit work is performed at the site. Exceptions apply to autonomous branches, divisions, and subsidiaries (Chapter 5).

**Public streets and sidewalks.** The free speech proviso in the U.S. Constitution establishes a right to picket on streets, sidewalks, and other public rights-of-way.[78] State and local authorities can, however, impose reasonable time, place, and manner restrictions.

Many localities prohibit picketers from obstructing the passage of pedestrians and vehicles. Other requirements may include permits, continuous motion, and a ban on profanity. Unions can challenge unreasonable restrictions on First Amendment grounds.[79]

**Driveways.** Public rights-of-way usually include a strip several feet wide on each side of the roadway. When a driveway crosses a public strip, the part of the driveway between the owner's property line and the street, the driveway "apron," is public property. The apron's dimensions can be ascertained by visiting the local public works department and asking for a road layout. The union can picket on the apron.

**Example:** Miller Furniture's warehouse is on a public road. A driveway runs from the plant to the road. Miller claims that it owns the entire driveway. However, a layout obtained from City Hall showed that the public right-of-way is 40-feet wide. Since the pavement is only 20-feet across, it appeared that land on one or both sides was

public property. Further checking confirmed dual public strips, including the first 10 feet of the company driveway.

**ULP charge.** When a driveway apron lies on public property, an employer violates the NLRA if it orders strikers to leave or asks police to make arrests for trespass.[80] The union should file a ULP charge.

---

### NLRB INTERFERENCE CHARGE

1. On June 19, 2013, Local 200 picketed the employer at its Cleveland facility as part of a lawful strike.
2. Union picketers patrolled on the apron of the plant driveway. The apron is a public right-of-way.
3. The employer falsely claimed to police that the pickets were on its property and the police forced the pickets to leave.
4. The employer is interfering with and restraining activity protected by the NLRA.
5. The employer's illegal actions have prolonged the strike.

---

**Employer-owned driveway.** If the employer owns the driveway, there is no public apron, and the union is ordered to leave, picketers should move to the nearest public sidewalk or street and the union should file a ULP charge seeking the right to picket on the driveway (see next page).

The NLRB can rule for the union if picketing on the nearest public way is too dangerous or distant to permit safe and effective appeals to non-strikers, customers, and delivery personnel.[81] The agency may deny access, however, if picketers have impeded persons or vehicles from entering.

**Pointer:** Research the legal owner of the property on which you want to picket. If the property is owned by a trust or other separate entity, the employer may not have sufficient authority to order strikers to leave.[82]

**Rented premises.** Some employers lease their quarters from industrial parks, shopping centers, or office buildings. If the property owner orders picketers to leave, file a ULP charge against the owner seeking a right to picket on the property. The NLRB applies a balancing test that considers several factors, including whether the premises are open to the public and whether picketing on a nearby street or sidewalk would be safe and effective.[83]

**Pointer:** Show a copy of the NLRB charge to the police. Ask that trespass arrests be deferred until the NLRB rules on the matter.

## Signs

Unions have considerable latitude in regard to picket signs, banners, and other publicity.

**Bloodsucker.** Picket signs usually focus on the issues in dispute. Still, nothing prevents the union from labeling an employer as a "union-buster," "criminal," "sweatshop operator," or "bloodsucker." An employer may not take action against a striker for expressing an opinion, however harsh.[84]

Employers sometimes harass picketers by suing for libel. Judges often dismiss the charges since an expression of opinion is not grounds for a lawsuit. As one judge explained, in a labor dispute "even seemingly 'factual' statements take on an appearance more closely resembling opinion than objective fact."[85]

A picketer or union that is sued for libel should file a ULP charge. The NLRB can order the employer to withdraw the suit and reimburse the defendant's legal expenses.[86]

## Conduct

Strikers have a right to approach linecrossers, hand out literature, and ask that they not enter—even if this causes a momentary traffic interruption.[87] Picketers can shout, use strong language, and gesture. But they cannot engage in violence, threats, property damage, or other egregious misbehavior. The following conduct goes over the line:

- Assaulting or threatening to assault a linecrosser (supervisor, non-striker, strike replacement, delivery driver, customer)
- Spitting on a linecrosser
- Placing tacks or nails on a driveway
- Kicking, scratching, or pounding a vehicle
- Blocking a person or vehicle from entering or leaving
- Throwing liquids, eggs, or rocks
- Pursuing a vehicle at high speed

• Brandishing a weapon

**Profanity.** Picketers can use strong language, including profanity, to demean linecrossers (other than customers or members of the

---

### PICKET LINE INSTRUCTIONS

1. The United States Constitution gives unions the right to picket and pass out handbills on public ways.

2. Section 7 of the *National Labor Relations Act* also guarantees the right to picket.

3. While picketing you may:

   • Ask persons to honor the line, even if they are not members of the bargaining unit.

   • Ask delivery persons not to enter.

   • Ask customers and the public not to patronize.

   • Hold up signs asking motorists to "Honk if you're with us."

   • Call strikebreakers "scabs."

4. Violence and threats are unlawful and can lead to termination. The employer may monitor your conduct through videotapes and sound recordings. Security guards may be instructed to provoke incidents. To protect your job and to safeguard the union:

   • Picket only where assigned by your picket captain.

   • Maintain peaceful and orderly picketing.

   • Cooperate with police officers and obey their instructions. If a problem arises, obtain the officer's name, department, and badge number. Report that information to your picket captain or the local.

   • Do not talk to strangers who hang around the picket line.

   • Picket in single file, keep moving, and maintain adequate spacing to allow vehicles and individuals to enter and leave. If a motor vehicle approaches, public.)[88] Discipline may be imposed, however, for repeated sexual, racial, or religious slurs directed at a particular individual.

**Civil disobedience.** Strikers who engage in peaceful nondisruptive

---

move out of the way.

- Do not use derogatory language regarding a person's race, ethnic origin, religion, gender, disability, age, or sexual orientation.
- Do not use profanity toward a customer or other member of the public.
- Do not threaten anyone with physical harm.
- Do not touch or crowd around persons or vehicles crossing the picket line.
- Do not interfere with traffic. Do not stop in front of a vehicle or walk in front of it more than once.
- Do not spit on anyone.
- Do not litter.
- Do not come to the picket line under the influence of alcohol or drugs. Do not bring alcohol, illegal substances, or weapons.
- If the employer establishes a "reserved gate" for contractors, do not picket that gate unless authorized by your picket captain.
- Report any incidents involving threatening or dangerous behavior by strikebreakers, supervisors, or guards to your picket captain or the local union. Make note of what happened (date, time, place, descriptions of individuals, witness names).
- Do not argue with other picketers. If a problem arises, talk to your picket captain.
- Refer reporters and others with questions to the union's designated spokesperson. Do not answer yourself.

5. If you have questions on how to conduct strike activities, speak with your picket captain or call the union.

civil disobedience do not lose NLRA protection. In one case, a Detroit newspaper fired eighteen strikers who were arrested after sitting down on company steps (after employees entered for the day). An NLRB judge ordered reinstatement with back pay, explaining that:

> The symbolic actions of those who sat down may have been technically illegal ... but so is parking overtime at a meter, and about as serious.[89]

## Shared worksite

When an employer shares a location with another business, the premises are called a "common situs." Examples include office buildings, construction sites, and shopping malls.

When picketing a shared worksite, the union must observe the following guidelines in order to limit the impact on secondary or "neutral" employers:

- The picket line should be located as close as possible to the struck employer.
- The struck employer's name should be printed on all picket signs.
- Picketers should be instructed not to interfere with deliveries to secondaries and not to induce work stoppages by secondary employees.[90]

**Note:** If a struck employer ceases operations at a shared worksite, the union can continue picketing if the employer stores equipment on the site or will resume operations when the strike concludes.[91]

**Separate gates.** The owner of a shared worksite can create a dual gate system to relieve pressure on secondaries. One entrance, usually in front, can be posted with a sign designating it as a "neutral" gate.

Another entrance, usually on the side or in the rear, can be designated as a "reserved" gate for employees, suppliers, visitors, and vendors of the struck employer. When a gate system is properly established, the union may only picket the reserved gate, even if it is far from public view.

If a person working for or delivering to the struck employer uses the neutral gate, the gate system is polluted and the union can picket the entrance. It must cease, however, if the property manager rehabilitates the system by posting new signs, issuing new instructions, or assigning guards to check identities.

**Note:** A gate system is not polluted if a vendor or contractor that provides services for the entire site, such as a food truck, uses the neutral gate.

**Tenant's gate.** A struck employer may create a "tenant's gate" for businesses that rent space on its premises. The union may not picket this entrance unless it is used by persons working for or servicing the struck employer or a tenant's employees are doing bargaining unit work.

## Targeting outside businesses

A striking union can conduct publicity campaigns against businesses that buy from the employer, furnish it with supplies, deliver its products, help it with financing, or assist it in other ways. Certain activities, however, are restricted.

**Picketing and other coercive activity.** Section 8(b)(4) of the NLRA, inserted by the *Taft-Hartley Act of 1947*, makes it illegal for a union to "threaten," "coerce," or "restrain" a secondary employer in order to stop it from doing business with a struck employer. This prevents the union from engaging in picketing, threats to picket, sit-ins, or large demonstrations.

Section 8(b)(4) also prohibits a union from inducing employees of a secondary employer to strike in solidarity, to refuse to handle struck products, or to refuse to perform services. An example would be asking dock workers not to load goods manufactured by a struck employer.

Both the struck employer and the secondary employer can file ULP charges if a union violates Section 8(b)(4). If the charge has merit, the NLRB is required to seek an immediate injunction in federal court.[92] The union can also be sued for damages.[93]

**Note:** Section 8(b)(4) does not apply at the premises of a strike-bound facility. Picketers can ask shippers, vendors, and contractors not to enter.[94] They can also address pleas to unions representing such workers.[95]

*Exceptions.* There are two exceptions to the ban on secondary picketing. As explained later, a union can picket:

- A retail establishment that is selling struck products (Chapter 4)
- An employer on whose premises strikebreakers are working (Chapter 7)

**Publicity activity.** Section 8(b)(4) does not prevent a union from using sharply-worded publicity to criticize and embarrass a secondary business and encourage customers to boycott. Protected activities include handbills, banners, and balloons (Chapter 9).

### Employer ULPs

An employer commits an unfair labor practice (ULP) if a manager, supervisor, guard, or other agent threatens or intimidates strikers or interferes with picketing. Violations can convert a walkout from an economic strike to an unfair labor practice strike (Chapter 13). Unlawful conduct includes:

- Filming workers engaged in orderly picketing, rallies, and other strike-related activities or writing down names
- Telling a striker that she will lose her job unless she returns to work
- Threatening to report strikers to the Department of Homeland Security
- Assaulting a striker, pushing a striker to the ground, or driving dangerously close to a picket line
- Brandishing a weapon in a threatening manner
- Threatening to harm a striker or a member of the striker's family
- Making a threatening gesture such as running a finger against a throat
- Parking heavy machinery or other equipment on sidewalks, streets, or public easements used by picketers
- Running a water sprinkler on picketers

- Asking police to arrest picketers for trespass without a reasonable concern that they are on the employer's property
- Threatening to fire a striker for name-calling or other minor misconduct
- Threatening to permanently subcontract bargaining unit work or close the facility
- Falsely informing strikers that permanent replacements have been hired.
- Pulling up union signs planted on public property
- Suggesting that strikers would be better off if they voted out the union
- Offering pay increases, promotions, or other benefits to induce a striker to return to work
- Refusing to bargain unless the union ends the strike

## Injunctions

If picketers are violent or block entrances, an employer can petition a state or federal judge to issue an injunction limiting the number, requiring them to walk several feet apart, or even forbidding patrolling altogether. Because a judge can enforce the order with fines and jail time, a court injunction can gravely damage a strike.

Employers often begin building for an injunction when a strike begins. Videographers may be hired in the hope of recording picket line violence. Security guards may be instructed to provoke strikers. A firm that specializes in strike security may induce non-strikers to sign affidavits.[96] Once a record is assembled, the employer files in court.

**Legal prerequisites.** The evidence needed for an injunction depends on the court system in which the employer files. The federal courts require an employer to prove that the union is responsible for unlawful acts, the acts are likely to continue, the police are unable or unwilling to provide adequate protection, the employer is complying with all of its legal obligations, and the employer is trying to resolve the dispute by negotiations, government mediation, or arbitration.[97] Some states and territories have similar requirements; others allow injunctions on lesser grounds.

**Avoiding an injunction.** To reduce the likelihood of a court injunction the union should:

- Meet with police before the strike, explain that the union's goals are peaceful, and provide the telephone numbers of union officials and the union attorney.
- Instruct strikers to avoid threats, blocking, and drinking on the picket line.
- Conduct training sessions for members and picket captains.
- Give picket captains the power to send unruly strikers home.
- Instruct picket captains to record employer provocations.
- Keep a log of misconduct by strikebreakers, security guards, and supervisors.
- Issue press releases and internet postings condemning violence.

**National emergency injunction.** In certain cases, the NLRA gives the President of the United States authority to seek a court order enjoining a strike for up to 80 days.[98] There must be a threat of a "national emergency" such as the shutdown of an entire coastal port system. During the stay, a federal board of inquiry briefs the President and the NLRB conducts a bargaining unit vote on the employer's final offer.

## Corporate campaigns

A corporate campaign is a no-holds-barred war on the employer, its parent entity, its sister branches, and its subsidiaries. Because of the scope, unions usually limit such campaigns to circumstances in which the union's survival is at risk. Corporate campaign tactics include:

- Communications conveying damaging information about the employer to creditors, Wall Street financial analysts, and the Securities and Exchange Commission[99]
- Broad consumer boycotts
- Class-action discrimination, overtime pay, and whistleblower lawsuits
- Pollution and hazardous waste complaints
- Requests for legislative hearings on company misconduct
- Opposition to tax exemptions, real estate abatements, building permits, licenses, and rate increases
- Boycott campaigns against businesses owned by stockholders, directors, and major customers

Corporate campaigns should be vetted by legal counsel. The employer may respond with a "RICO lawsuit" charging the union with extortion. Though the suit will probably fail, it can burden the union with legal expenses.

# Questions and Answers

### Quick retreat

Q. Three days after we struck a California steel company, the president called the state labor mediation agency. He says the agency has no record of receiving a labor dispute notice from the union. What should we do?

A. This depends. If you have a return receipt or other proof of service, you are secure. Otherwise, call off the strike and offer to return. Employees who are allowed back to work cannot be disciplined.[100] After they return, you can serve the mediation agency, wait 30 days, and resume the strike.

### State law

Q. A law in our state says unions must give 15 days notice before striking. Is the law binding?

A. Not in workplaces covered by the *National Labor Relations Act*. The NLRA preempts state laws that conflict with its provisions.[101]

### Threat to withdraw agreements

Q. We told the company's lead negotiator that we would be taking a strike vote in three days. He responded that if we struck, he would withdraw all of his tentative agreements and that bargaining would have to "start from scratch." Can he do this?

A. No. An employer may not withdraw from tentative agreements without good cause. A strike does not automatically supply such grounds.[102] File an NLRB charge against the threat.

### Strike poll

Q. We sent a hospital a 10-day strike notice. Management is taking a poll to see which employees will be taking part. Is this allowed?

A. Yes, with conditions. An employer may poll employees if it has a reasonable basis to fear an imminent strike and it needs information to decide whether to stay open.[103] The employer must advise each employee of the reason for the inquiry, explain that participation is voluntary, and guarantee that there will be no reprisals for expressing an intention to strike.[104]

### Progressive walkout

Q. Does a union have to take the entire bargaining unit out on the first day of a strike?

A. No. A union can call a rolling strike, with one group going out at a time.[105]

### Delivery gate

Q. The day after we began our strike, guards put a sign on a side entrance stating: "Neutral Gate — Reserved for Deliveries." Can we picket the gate?

A. Yes. An employer cannot create a reserved gate for deliveries related to its regular operations.

### Contractor's gate

Q. Can an employer create a reserved gate for contractors during a strike?

**A.** Yes, if the contractors are:

- Performing work that is unrelated to the employer's regular operations, for example, constructing an addition. Contractors that are overhauling equipment, renovating existing structures, providing temporary labor, making deliveries, or performing security functions cannot use the gate.[106]

- Performing work that, if carried out when the facility was operating regularly, would not require a partial or total curtailment of operations.

**Pointer:** When investigating whether a business is qualified to use a contractor's gate, request that the employer furnish job orders, blueprints, and other relevant documents. If the documents are inconclusive, request access to the facility to observe the work.[107]

**Note:** The rule insulating a contractor's gate does not apply at a construction site.[108]

### Police

**Q.** The police say that they will make arrests unless the picket line immediately separates when a delivery truck approaches. Any suggestions?

**A.** Remind them that the NLRA affords strikers a protected right to briefly approach persons crossing the picket line to hand out literature and plead the union's case.[109] Ask for a short period, such as 30 seconds or a minute, before having to step back.

### Mass picketing

**Q.** Do we risk ULP charges if all 185 union members picket simultaneously?

A. Possibly. If the number of picketers is extremely large relative to the width of the sidewalk, the NLRB or a court may find an NLRA violation on the ground that a person intending to work would be intimidated.[110] Mass picketing may be deemed lawful, however, if the line forms gaps to allow non-strikers to pass.[111]

### Employer reduces offer

Q. Can an employer lower its wage and benefit offer or add new demands during a strike?

A. Yes. Neither party is required to freeze its bargaining position. The employer may decide that strike losses warrant a lower economic offer. Or it may decide that with permanent replacements on board it needs to remove union security provisions from the contract.[112]

### Charge against union

Q. The company has filed ULP charges against the union claiming that picketers are threatening linecrossers, blocking deliveries, and damaging cars. Is the union responsible for the actions of its members? What are the possible penalties?

A. Unions have a duty to control their picket lines. In the event of violence or threats of violence, the NLRB can find the union at fault and issue a desist order. The NLRB does not issue fines. Nor does it prosecute individuals.

### Plate numbers

Q. Can we photograph the license plates of scab trucks?

A. Yes, but you may not publish the numbers or use them to find drivers' home addresses.[113]

### Employer videotaping

**Q.** Although our strike has been totally peaceful, management is videotaping us all day. Should we file a ULP charge?

**A.** Yes. Employer videotaping is coercive.[114] It is only lawful if picketers have engaged in violence, blocking, trespass, or other serious misconduct. Even in such circumstances, the employer may not photograph strikers talking among themselves or relaxing away from the picket line.[115]

### Backpedal

**Q.** Strikers are talking about returning to work. To avoid defeat, we are thinking of accepting the employer's final contract proposal which we turned down two weeks ago. If we do so, will the employer be bound?

**A.** This depends. If a union acts within a reasonable time, it can change its mind and accept the employer's latest contract offer.[116]

The acceptance can be rejected, however, if, during the interim, the employer withdrew the offer, made a new offer, or announced that a new offer would be made.

### Crass warfare

Q. A supervisor called a picketer a "f***ing a**hole." Unfair labor practice?

A. Probably not. Run-of-the-mill profanity is allowed during strikes. But racial, ethnic, or sexual slurs, uttered frequently, may be ruled unlawful.[117]

### Junk mail

Q. Can the company mail letters to strikers characterizing the union's bargaining demands as "thoughtless and irresponsible."

A. Yes. An employer may criticize the union's bargaining position. It only commits a ULP if it impugns the integrity of union leaders or tries to pit one part of the bargaining unit against another.[118]

### Home invasion

Q. Can a supervisor call a striker at home and ask her to return to work?

A. Yes, unless the supervisor offers a pay increase, promotion, extra seniority, or other term or condition in excess of what the employer offered the union at the bargaining table.[119]

### Violence by union officer

Q. A union officer got in a fight and broke a scab's nose. Could this affect the officer's ability to hold union office?

**A.** Yes. The federal *Landrum-Griffin Act* bars persons convicted of serious crimes from serving as union officers or representatives.[120] The listed offenses include an "assault which inflicts grievous bodily injury."

### Subcontract

**Q.** Can an employer permanently outsource bargaining unit work during a strike?

**A.** Not necessarily. A struck employer may only enter into a long-term or permanent contract that will displace unit employees after a strike if it has a substantial business justification — for example, an inability to hire a contractor to perform the work on a temporary basis.[121] Moreover, the employer must give the union prior notice of its plan and, if the union requests, bargain to impasse on the decision and its effects.[122] Permanently outsourcing bargaining unit work can convert an economic strike to a ULP strike, even if the employer does not reveal its intentions until after employees return to their jobs.[123]

> **Note:** A struck employer has no obligation to bargain before making temporary arrangements to outsource unit work.[124] Nor is it required to engage in decisional bargaining if the change is necessitated by a permanent and fundamental change in the nature of the enterprise.[125]

> **Pointer:** Submit periodic requests for contracts, correspondence, and e-mail between the employer and contractors performing bargaining unit work.

### Shutdown

**Q.** In the second month of our strike, the company announced that it was closing the plant for good. Doesn't it have to pay us 60 days wages under WARN, the federal plant closing law?

A. No. The WARN law does not apply to strike-related closings.

### Workers' compensation

Q. A picketer fell and broke her ankle. Can she collect workers' compensation?

A. No. Workers' compensation does not cover strikers' injuries.

### State sabotage

Q. The state unemployment insurance (UI) office is referring persons to work as scabs during our strike. Can we do anything about it?

A. Make a stink. Federal rules prohibit UI agencies from making referrals to workplaces that are on strike or locked out.[126]

### General strike

Q. We have been locked out for six months. Can unions in the area support us by calling a general strike like they did in the 1930's?

A. Not safely. For one thing, most unions today are subject to contracts prohibiting sympathy strikes. For another, the *Taft-Hartley Act of 1947* forbids unions from striking a neutral employer if the goal or likely consequence is a cessation of business between the neutral and other entities such as suppliers and customers.[127]

### Property damage

Q. Someone destroyed a company electrical tower. Can the company sue the union?

A. Not without evidence of responsibility. A union is not liable for property losses during a strike unless it authorized, ratified, or approved the actions in question.[128]

FRANK DAWSON AT HOME

THE UNION'S PICKETING LIQUOR STORES, ASKING SHOPPERS NOT TO BUY COORS BEER—

—BECAUSE MY TRUCKS DELIVER IT!

AND MY USELESS LAWYER SAYS THERE'S NOTHING I CAN DO!

# 4

# Consumer Picketing

*Guidelines* ◆ *Shopping centers*

**P**ICKETING STORES THAT SELL the employer's products can publicize a strike and affect earnings. It is a good way to generate community support. Although the NLRA generally bars unions from picketing secondary employers (pages 55–56), exceptions apply to retail stores and distributors provided the union only asks the public not to buy struck products.[129] The union may not ask customers to stop doing all business with a store. Nor may it demand that a store cease buying products from the struck employer.

**Note:** Struck products include items that the struck employer manufactures, processes, distributes, or enhances in value.[130]

## Guidelines

A union that conducts consumer picketing should heed the following guidelines to avoid an NLRB charge that it is trying to coerce a store or distributor:

**Name the struck employer and its products.** Picket signs and handbills should clearly identify the struck employer and the targeted products and explain what action the union wants customers to take. "Budweiser workers on strike—Boycott Bud" conveys the necessary information. "Boycott scab beer" does not. On the bottom add: "This is not a strike or boycott against this store."

**Do not induce store employees.** Picketers should not ask store employees to stop handling struck products or to go on strike against the store. Picketing should be confined to hours when the seller is open for business and should not take place in front of entrances reserved exclusively for store employees. The best practice is to avoid conversations with store personnel.

**Do not picket if struck products are the predominant or only items being sold.** Consumer picketing is unlawful if struck goods provide all or the bulk of a seller's income. For example, a union on strike against Chevron Oil Company cannot picket independently owned Chevron gas stations. Nor may it ask shoppers to boycott an item that is so merged with other products—for example, plastic bags at a grocery store—that compliance would cripple the seller.

**Note:** While a union cannot picket in the above circumstances, it can distribute handbills and display stationary banners. Since it is not picketing, it can urge customers to boycott the entire store (see Chapter 9).

---

## INSTRUCTIONS FOR CONSUMER PICKETERS

Our goal in picketing stores is to encourage consumers to boycott _____ Company products. The National Labor Relations Act protects consumer picketing if picketers obey the following instructions:

1. Picket in a peaceful manner. Do not engage in altercations, arguments, or misconduct of any kind.

2. Picket customer entrances only. If the store is at the rear of a parking lot, or inside a mall, picket on the sidewalk immediately in front of the store. If the owner or its agent tells you to leave because the property is private, move to the nearest location on public property. In such cases, the union may file NLRB charges seeking more direct access.

3. Do not picket entrances set aside for employees or deliveries. Do not converse with store employees or delivery drivers and do not interfere with their work.

4. Do not tell passers-by that the store is unfair or being struck. Do not ask customers to boycott the entire store. Only ask that they not buy struck products.

5. Do not ask store owners or managers to stop selling struck products.

6. Be courteous. If customers drop handbills on the ground, pick them up and keep the area clean.

7. Do not use intoxicating beverages while on duty. Do not have such beverages on your person.

8. If any persons complain about your picketing, tell them that you have your instructions and that they should register a complaint with the union.

---

## Shopping centers

When a store is located in a shopping center, it may be difficult to get close enough to display signs and distribute flyers. As a general rule, a shopping center can bar a union from picketing or handing out leaflets on its property. An exception arises, if the center regularly allows other organizations—for example, the Salvation Army or the Little League—to set up tables or give out literature. In such circumstances, the union may be able to gain access by filing an NLRB charge against the property owner.[131]

# Questions and Answers

### Newspaper strike

Q. We are on strike against a newspaper. Can we picket department stores to ask the public not to buy products advertised in the paper?

A. Yes. The advertised items are struck products because the newspaper is enhancing their value. Be sure to identify the items on your signs and in your handbills.

### Pepsi's the one

Q. Our company makes aluminum cans for Pepsi-Cola. Can we picket stores that sell Pepsi?

A. Yes, if your signs are limited to appeals not to buy Pepsi in cans.

### Laundry workers

Q. We launder table linen for local restaurants. Can we picket these establishments?

**A.** Yes, but you cannot ask patrons to buy meals elsewhere.

### Threat to picket

**Q.** We are on strike against a meatpacking company. Can we tell grocery store managers that we will picket if they continue selling the company's products?

**A.** Yes, but make clear that picketers will only ask customers to boycott the struck products.

### State law

**Q.** A law in our state forbids picketing at workplaces where no strike is in progress. Does this prevent consumer picketing?

**A.** No. The NLRA supesedes conflicting state laws.

# 5

# Striking Allied Enterprises

*Single enterprise allies* ◆ *Struck work allies* ◆
*Foreign entities*

THE TAFT-HARTLEY BAN on secondary picketing does not apply to "allies" of a struck employer. A union can picket an allied enterprise with on-strike signs, ask employees to stop working, and attempt to turn away deliveries.[132] Who are allies? A commonsense listing would include branches and subsidiaries of the struck employer, financing institutions, and major suppliers and customers. Unfortunately, the authorities take a far more narrow approach, limiting the designation of allies to 1) entities that are so integrated with the struck employer that they form a "single" enterprise, and 2) entities that are performing struck work.

## Single enterprise allies

The NLRB asks four questions to decide whether two entities form a single enterprise:

1. Are the entities under common ownership or financial control?
2. Are their day-to-day labor relations activities commonly or centrally controlled?
3. Are their operations interrelated?
4. Are they under common management?

**Applying the factors.** Common ownership or financial control is essential for a single enterprise. Common or centralized labor relations is also required. If a subsidiary independently determines its wage rates, work rules, and labor policies, it is not part of a single enterprise. There must also be some degree of interrelatedness between the entities such as joint purchases, shared employees, or common inventories. Common management is the least essential factor; its presence suggests a single enterprise but its absence is not fatal.

> **Example:** Huttig Door Co. owned branches in Montana and South Carolina. South Carolina went on strike. Huttig centrally supervised labor relations at both facilities but management was separate. Montana supplied 50 to 60 per cent of South Carolina's components and the branches exchanged equipment. Ruling that the branches

were part of a single enterprise, the NLRB allowed strikers from the South Carolina branch to picket the Montana facility.[133]

**Example:** The Hearst Corporation owned newspapers in Los Angeles and San Francisco. Both papers had authority to decide their wages and work rules. Headquarters gave advice on collective bargaining but did not participate in negotiations or approve contracts. Although the entities were commonly owned, and there was some interrelatedness, the NLRB found them to be substantially autonomous. Strikers at the Los Angeles paper could not picket in San Francisco.[134]

**Cautions.** There is always a risk when a union pickets a branch or subsidiary. Although common ownership may be apparent, the entity may be operating autonomously, especially in regard to labor relations. In such circumstances, the union could be sued for damages. Before setting up a picket line, the union should gather as much information as possible and discuss the matter with its attorney.

Even when ally status is crystal clear, the union must consider the impact on workers at the allied enterprise. If they are subject to a collective bargaining agreement that prohibits sympathy strikes, honoring a picket line could lead to discharges. If their union advises them not to work, it could be sued for breach of contract. In one case, meat packers on strike in Iowa picketed a corporate branch in South Dakota. When the union representing the South Dakota employees instructed its members to honor the picket line, the South Dakota branch sued it and won a $24.6 million judgment.

### Struck work allies

To keep customers from bolting, a struck employer may ask an outside business to temporarily fill its commitments. Under the

NLRA, a business that takes on struck work is considered an ally, allowing the union to picket with on-strike signs.

**Who made the arrangement?** In order for an ally relationship to come about, the struck employer must make the arrangements.[135] If a customer searches out a new supplier or service provider, the business that steps in is not an ally.

> **Example:** Mama's Pizza traditionally buys its dough from Tasty Bakery. When the workers at Tasty went on strike, Mama contracted with another bakery. Can the Tasty union picket this bakery? No, because the customer, not Tasty, made the arrangements.

**Identifying struck work allies.** A union that suspects that its employer is farming out work can insist that the employer furnish the names of businesses doing bargaining unit work, relevant contracts, and correspondence. According to the NLRB: "A bargaining representative is entitled to information as to whether and to what extent during a strike or lockout, the employer is using outside firms to perform unit work."[136]

## Foreign entities

Members may suggest sending strikers to picket a foreign branch or subsidiary. The Taft-Hartley Act, however, bars U.S. unions from conducting secondary picketing throughout the globe. If the foreign branch administers its labor relations policies free of close supervision from the U.S., it is not an ally.

**International solidarity.** Can a U.S. union avoid Taft-Hartley by asking a foreign union to picket in its place? In a 1993 case, the NLRB said no, reasoning that a union that responds to another union's request is an agent of that union.[137] On appeal, a federal circuit court reversed, stating:

> We discern nothing in the law of agency to support a theory transforming one union into the agent of another based upon the spirit of labor solidarity standing alone.[138]

Despite the reversal, the NLRB has not modified its dubious agency theory. Consequently, unless a foreign entity clearly meets the definition of an ally, a union seeking picketing assistance should do so discretely and should not take part in the planning or the execution.

# Questions and Answers

### Struck work

Q. Our company is farming out work to a company with four locations but only one is doing our work. Can we picket all four locations?

A. Not safely. A Board ruling appears to restrict picketing to locations where struck work is being performed.[139]

### Temp agency

Q. Labor Ready is supplying temporary workers during our strike. Can we picket its local office?

A. Yes, because they are sending employees to do your work.[140]

### Bus company

Q. Can we picket the headquarters of a bus company that is driving scabs into the plant?

**A.** No. An entity does not become an ally simply by providing a service to a struck enterprise.

### College campus

**Q.** We are on strike against a company that operates a restaurant on a college campus. Can we picket the college administration building?

**A.** Not safely. Unless college employees are doing your work, the college is not an ally.

### Government agency

**Q.** We are striking a trucking company that operates under contract with a county transportation authority. Can we picket the authority's office?

**A.** No. Picketing a government agency violates Section 8(b)(4) unless the agency is directly and intimately involved in the labor dispute.[141]

# 6

## Making it Personal

PICKETING THE HOME OF AN OWNER, director, trustee, or stockholder is a way to personalize a labor struggle. The NLRA protects peaceful residential picketing even if it causes annoyance and embarrassment to family members.[142] Employees cannot be disciplined for participating. Employers cannot discipline employees for participating. The only impediments are local laws.

Ordinances in some cities and towns forbid picketing before a single residence. The union can usually avoid such a law by running the line down the entire block.[143] Some localities ban picketing within a particular number of feet from a targeted residence. If the distance is modest, the union must observe it. If it is excessive—for example, 200 feet—the union can challenge it under the First Amendment.[144]

---

### RESIDENTIAL PICKETING INSTRUCTIONS

The following Do's and Don'ts are for residential picketing. Some are dictated by law, some by courtesy and practicality. We will ask persons who fail to honor these instructions not to participate. We appreciate your cooperation. Remember: we are only picketing to publicize our labor dispute.

#### DO'S:

- **Do** follow the union's leadership.
- **Do** walk single or double file in an orderly fashion.
- **Do** cooperate with the police.

#### DON'TS:

- **Don't** yell, chant, sing loudly, or call anyone names.
- **Don't** picket solely in front of a particular home or residence.
- **Don't** stand or walk on private property.
- **Don't** block or interfere with anyone who wants to enter or exit.
- **Don't** argue with neighbors or passers-by.
- **Don't** bring alcohol, weapons, or illegal drugs.
- **Don't** talk with children.
- **Don't** litter.
- **Don't** create a road hazard or traffic jam or park where prohibited.

---

Arizona, Arkansas, Hawaii, Illinois, and Virginia ban picketing "before or about the residence or dwelling place of any individual." Michigan, Minnesota, and Nebraska have similar laws. Unions in these states should consult with counsel.

**Conduct.** Picketing should not include vulgar language, excessive noise, or threats. Avoid conversations with neighborhood children.

**Signs and handbills.** Picket signs and handbills can describe the reasons for the strike, condemn the employer's policies, list the target's name and telephone number, and urge neighbors to register their support.

**Injunctions.** Homeowners can seek court injunctions against residential picketing, claiming nuisance or breach of privacy. Judges sometimes cooperate, especially when picketing is raucous or prolonged.

# 7

# Ambulatory Picketing

*Picketing rules* ◆ *Further precautions*

THE UNION CAN PICKET any location where an employee of a struck employer is working—even on the premises of a secondary employer. "Ambulatory" picketing is a lawful means to confront strike replacements, non-strikers, supervisors, and managers.

### Picketing rules

When picketing a strikebreaker who is temporarily working on the premises of a secondary employer, the union must heed four rules called the *Moore Dry Dock* standards.[145]

1. **Only picket when the strikebreaker is on the secondary's premises.**
Picketing must not begin before the scab arrives or continue after
the scab departs.

   **Pointer:** To create an opportunity to charge the union with secondary picketing, a secondary may instruct a scab to sneak out through
   a rear exit. To foil the scheme, assign an observer to watch the exit
   and report when the scab departs.

2. **Only picket if the scab is engaged in the struck employer's normal
operations.** The union cannot picket a hotel simply because a
scab is staying for the night.

3. **Picket as close as possible to where the scab is working, with due
regard for property rights and reserve gates.** Ask the secondary
employer for permission to enter the premises and picket near
where the scab is working. If the secondary denies the request (as
is likely), the union can picket the nearest entrance.[146] If the secondary designates a special entrance for employees of the struck
employer, the union must confine its picketing to that gate.

4. **Put the struck employer's name on all picket signs.** Do not list the
secondary's name. In small letters, write: "This picket is not
intended to induce employees of other businesses to cease work."
Signs that simply say "On strike" or "Unfair" are inadequate.

## Further precautions

Compliance with the *Dry Dock* standards does not mean picketing
is home free. The union must also avoid other conduct that suggests
an intent to pressure the secondary or induce its employees to strike.
To this end, picketers should not:

- Ask employees of the secondary to stop work.
- Call secondary employees "scabs."
- Ask customers or delivery persons to respect the picket line.
- Record the names or licence plate numbers of secondary employees, including delivery drivers.

See instructions for ambulatory picketing on next page.

**Silence is not golden.** If a secondary employee asks a picketer why the union is patrolling, the picketer should give an answer. The NLRB may view silence as a signal to stop work. The best response is to point to a picket sign or a union flyer and say, "This explains."

### PICKET SIGN

## TEAMSTERS
## LOCAL 728

### ON STRIKE AGAINST DAWSON
### TRUCKING FOR UNFAIR
### LABOR PRACTICES

This picketing is not directed toward the employees
of any other employer.

## AMBULATORY PICKETING INSTRUCTIONS

The *National Labor Relations Act* (NLRA) permits us to picket Dawson Trucking not only at its principal place of business but wherever its employees are doing bargaining unit work. This is called "ambulatory picketing." Local 728 has no dispute with any other employer. To avoid charges that the union is trying to coerce a neutral employer or to induce employees of other employers to strike, please carefully follow these instructions:

• If you are certain that a Dawson driver is present at the job site, you or the picket captain must hand deliver a letter directed to the manager of the building or terminal. The letter will ask that you be permitted to enter the premises so that you may picket the Dawson truck and driver as closely as possible.

• The letter should be presented to someone in authority — a manager, a supervisor or a front gate guard. Do not engage in conversation. During this time there should be no picketing or milling about the site.

• If the customer gives you permission, enter the site and picket as closely as possible to the Dawson truck and driver. Do not picket anywhere else on the property.

## NOTICE TO THE PUBLIC

Teamsters Local 728 is on strike against Dawson Trucking. We have no dispute with any other company at this location.

Drivers working for Dawson spend much of their time away from Dawson's premises. This makes it necessary for us to picket where they are working. We are picketing here because Dawson drivers are present.

This picketing is directed only at Dawson drivers and is not an appeal for any other workers to stop work.

---

If you are refused permission, picket the entrance closest to where you believe the scab is working. If the customer establishes a reserve gate for Dawson employees, picket that gate only and call the union.

The union will give you a picket sign that will make clear that your picketing is directed at Dawson. Do not use other signs.

Do not call persons other than Dawson employees "scabs" or ask them to honor the union picket line.

Make way for any vehicles or persons entering or leaving the premises.

Do not converse with terminal or customer employees or employees of other businesses — not even to say "good morning."

Do not engage in any violence, arguments, or misconduct of any kind. Such conduct may be used as an excuse to take legal action against you or Local 728.

Do not come to the picket line under the influence of alcohol or drugs. Do not have any alcohol, illegal substances, or weapons on your person.

If someone asks about the picketing, point to your sign and state that it speaks for itself. Do not wink or give any other signal to stop work.

Close the picket line when the Dawson driver completes his or her business and leaves for the day.

# Questions and Answers

### Trailing

Q. Can we follow scabs as they travel to outside work locations?

A. Yes, but you must not tailgate, crowd, or engage in other intimidating conduct.

### Refusal to work behind a picket line

Q. We picketed a scab while he worked at a construction site. Several union workers at the site stopped working. Can we be sued for causing a secondary strike?

**A.** Not if you followed the *Dry Dock* standards and did not ask or signal anyone to stop work. An ambulatory picket line does not lose its protected status because secondary employees refuse to work behind it.[147]

### Lunch hour

**Q.** When scabs stop work for lunch, do we have to stop patrolling?

**A.** No. Ambulatory picketing can continue during meal, rest, or other temporary breaks.[148]

### Request not to unload

**Q.** We are picketing stores while company trucks make deliveries. Can we ask store workers not to unload the trucks?

**A.** Yes, with care. Ambulatory picketers can ask secondary employees not to perform services that aid the struck employer, such as unloading goods.[149] You cannot ask the workers to stop work entirely or to refuse to handle products after they are unloaded.

**Threat to picket**

Q. We are striking a company that sends technicians to other employers. Can we warn these businesses that we will picket if a scab enters their facility?

A. Yes, but make clear that you will conform to the *Moore Dry Dock* standards. For instance, you might send a letter warning: "If an employee of _____ enters your premises to perform services, we will picket as closely as possible to his or her work."

# 8
# Honor Thy Line

*Nonunion workers* ◆ *Union workers*

A N EMPLOYEE WHO HONORS a picket line is called a "sympathy striker." A person who refuses to do a striker's job is also a member of this illustrious family. Different legal considerations apply to union and nonunion workers.

## Nonunion workers

The rights of a nonunion worker to respect a union picket line are contradictory. On the one hand, the *National Labor Relations Act*

*(NLRA)* says the activity is protected and prohibits an employer from taking adverse action.[150] On the other hand, the Act allows the employer to hire a permanent replacement to take over the sympathy striker's job. Although the employer must give the sympathy striker a preferential right to fill future vacancies, there is often little difference between being permanently replaced and being fired.

An employer is not allowed to permanently replace a sympathy striker if the strike being honored was caused by an unfair labor practice (see Chapter 13). Even then, however, it may take years of litigation to vindicate the striker's rights.

## Union workers

Assume two unions in a workplace, Union A and Union B. If Union A hits the bricks, can workers represented by Union B safely honor Union A's picket line? Another scenario: a union truck driver is assigned to deliver to a struck facility. If the driver honors the picket line, is he or she at risk?

Determining whether a union worker can safely honor a picket line usually requires a careful examination of the contract covering the worker, especially any clauses relating to sympathy strikes. The most common formulations are "express ban," "express authorization," and "ambiguous rights."

**Express ban.** Contract language such as the following expressly bans sympathy strikes:

> The union agrees that there shall be no strike of any kind, including a sympathy strike, slowdown, stoppage of work, sickout, sit-in, or delay of work during the term of this agreement.

This provision gives up ("waives") the NLRA right to honor a picket line. Transgression is grounds for discharge. If the union encourages its members to honor a line, the employer could sue it for breach of contract.

There are two scenarios in which the law nullifies a contractual ban on sympathy strikes. The first is where a *serious* unfair labor practice precipitates the strike being honored.[151] Serious unfair labor practices are those that are "destructive of the foundation on which collective bargaining must rest."[152] Examples include discriminatory discharges and refusals to bargain. In these circumstances, a no-sympathy-strike clause is not effective unless the contract expressly bans unfair labor practice strikes.

The second exception is based on Section 502 of the NLRA. This law says that a refusal to perform duties "because of abnormally dangerous conditions for work ... [shall not] ... be deemed a strike."[153] Refusing to cross a picket line because of a fear of personal harm can fall under Section 502 if there have been threats or assaults on the line.[154]

**Express authorization.** Some collective bargaining agreements, especially in the transportation sector, expressly recognize the right to honor picket lines. For example, Article 9 of the Teamsters' National Master Freight Agreement reads:

> It shall not be a violation of this agreement and it shall not be cause for discharge, disciplinary action, or permanent replacement in the event an employee refuses to enter upon any property involving a primary labor dispute, or refuses to go through or work behind any primary picket line, including the primary picket line of unions party to this agreement, and including picket lines at the employer's place of business.

Article 9 allows Teamster freight drivers to respect lawful picket lines at their place of employment and at locations where they are assigned to deliver or pick up. Employers may not impose discipline. Nor may they hire permanent replacements. Teamster contracts with United Parcel Service (UPS) have similar language.

The Master Freight and UPS contracts are a boon to striking unions because they give many delivery drivers a license to honor picket lines. Yet it can be a mistake to assume too much. Not all Teamster bargaining agreements have clauses like Article 9. Some drivers are unaware of their rights or lack sympathy for strikers. Finally, it is common for a driver to arrive at a picketed facility, call dispatch to register an objection, and receive instructions to wait until a supervisor can drive the truck through the line.

**Pointer:** The union should give formal notice of its strike to the local Teamsters union and Teamsters joint council.

**Ambiguous rights.** Many no-strike clauses are silent about sympathy strikes. For example, the clause may read as follows:

There shall be no strike, stoppage, slowdown, picketing, or lockout during the term of this agreement.

This type of clause is open to opposing interpretations. The employer can assert that it bars all strikes, including sympathy strikes. The union can assert that the omission of the term "sympathy strike" suggests an intent to permit the activity.

If the issue is taken to arbitration or the NLRB, the union's position will be supported by a history of workers honoring picket lines without adverse consequences and by failed attempts by the employer to bargain an express ban on sympathy strikes. The employer will have a good case if it has historically disciplined employees for respecting picketlines or if the union tried and failed to win contractual language recognizing the right to engage in sympathy strikes.

# Questions and Answers

### Expired contract

Q. Our contract, which prohibits sympathy strikes, expired two weeks ago. We are bargaining over a new agreement. If another union in our facility hits the bricks, can we honor its picket line?

A. Yes. The contract's strike restrictions are no longer in effect.[155]

### Hospital union

Q. Does a union that represents hospital workers have to give advance notice before honoring another union's picket line?

A. Yes. Unions that honor picket lines at health care institutions must give 10 days written notice to the institution and the Federal Mediation and Conciliation Service (FMCS).[156] The 10-day rule also applies to a non-healthcare union that honors or joins a picket line at a health care institution.[157]

### Escaping judgement

Q. The company is suing the union for $2 million because it honored another union's picket line. If the company wins, could it attach the union's future dues collections?

A. Theoretically, yes, although the union may be able to escape the debt by filing for bankruptcy.[158]

# Secondary Boycotts

*Handbilling* ◆ *Bannering* ◆ *Ballooning*

IT SOMETIMES COMES AS A SURPRISE to learn that unions can organize boycotts and other campaigns against persons and businesses not directly party to labor disputes. Section 8(b)(4) of the *National Labor Relations Act (NLRA)* bans unions from "threatening," "restraining," or "coercing" secondary employers. But in a landmark 1988 ruling, the U.S. Supreme Court said this language only bars *confrontational* activities such as picketing, disruption, and vio-

## INSTRUCTIONS FOR HANDING OUT FLYERS AT A SECONDARY EMPLOYER

The *National Labor Relations Act* and the U.S. Constitution guarantee unions, members, and supporters the right to handbill businesses that trade with a struck employer, provide it with services, sell its products, or help it in other ways. We may ask customers and the public to support our struggle by boycotting the secondary's products or services. *However, the law does not allow us to engage in picketing or picket-like activities.* Please follow the instructions below.

### DO'S

- **Do** hand out your flyers in a courteous and professional manner.
- **Do** refer people who ask questions to an appropriate union representative.
- **Do** pick up discarded leaflets.
- **Do** obey orders from law enforcement officials.

### DON'TS

- **Don't** walk back and forth or act in any manner that could be construed as picketing.
- **Don't** congregate in groups; no more than one or two handbillers should stand at a door or entrance.
- **Don't** mill around without handbills.
- **Don't** hold signs.
- **Don't** talk to employees of the secondary or hand them flyers.
- **Don't** get into arguments with customers.
- **Don't** force handbills on anyone.
- **Don't** block entrances or exits.
- **Don't** go inside the secondary's premises.
- **Don't** shout, use profanity, threaten violence, or call people names.
- **Don't** advise anyone to stop work. If a driver asks whether he or she should make a delivery to the facility, say yes.
- **Don't** threaten to picket. Don't even use the word.
- **Don't** videotape customers or employees.

lence.[159] The ruling allows unions to use less confrontational publicity techniques—for example, handbilling, bannering, and ballooning—to deter secondary employers from aiding or doing business with a primary employer.[160] As long as the union directs its message to the secondary, its customers, and the general public, and does not ask the secondary's employees to strike or to stop working, it can carry out a hard-hitting campaign.

Potential secondary targets include customers, suppliers, contractors, delivery companies, shippers, banks, landlords, members of the employer's corporate family, and businesses owned or managed by stockholders, directors, and trustees. Flyers and other union literature can condemn these entities, attack their products and services, expose current or past illegalities, and ask the public to withhold patronage.

For example, a hospital union can take measures against a business owned by a hospital trustee. The union can use handbills, advertisements, and stationary banners to expose the way the business treats its employees or carries out unethical practices. The union can highlight past illegalities, ask customers to boycott, and notify the secondary that the campaign will continue until the hospital signs a fair contract.[161]

## Handbilling

Flyers attacking a secondary can be distributed on streets and sidewalks, in parks, and outside stadiums and arenas. In some cases the union can assert distribution rights on private sidewalks and concourses, for example when a shopping mall regularly allows civic groups or charities to solicit on its property.[162]

**Conduct.** Union handbillers can approach pedestrians and drivers. They may wear T-shirts with messages or appeals. They may not, however, walk in circles, hold flyers over their heads like picket signs, gather in groups, ask employees to stop working, or interfere with deliveries.

**Content.** Union handbills should explain the relationship between the targeted business and the struck employer. The explanation can be brief, for example: "This company does business with _____, an employer that refuses to negotiate a fair contract with its employees." The flyer should include the following: "Our appeal is directed to the general public. We are not asking any person to refuse to work or deliver goods."

**Example:** A California union was in a labor dispute with a cleaning contractor whose biggest customer was Delta Airlines. To pressure Delta to use its influence, the union distributed flyers at airline terminals. One side said: "Please do not fly Delta Airlines. Delta Airlines unfair, does not provide AFL-CIO conditions of employment." The other side listed Delta's accident record and warned:

"It takes more than money to fly Delta. It takes nerve."

Delta filed Section 8(b)(4) charges against the union but the NLRB ruled that the handbilling was lawful.[163]

**Pointer:** Publicity materials are most effective when they expose illegal or unethical business practices. Research the secondary and its officials through the Better Business Bureau, city inspection departments, and the NLRB website. Illegal conduct, even years in the past, can provide a basis for an eye-catching headline such as "Tax Cheater," "Lawbreaker," or "Criminal."

## Bannering

Unions can hold large stationary banners or billboards outside the premises of a secondary.[164] Bannering is not picketing or tantamount to picketing if holders stay in place and do not interfere with

---

### BANNERING INSTRUCTIONS

The National Labor Relations Act and the U.S. Constitution guarantee our right as union members involved in a labor dispute to hold banners outside businesses that trade with our employer, service it, sell its products, or help it in other ways. We may also pass out leaflets. We may not, however, engage in picketing or picket-like activities. Please follow the instructions below.

#### DO'S

- **Do** hold your banner completely stationary.
- **Do** stand on public sidewalks or rights-of-way, not private property.
- **Do** position the banner so that it faces traffic.
- **Do** be peaceful, without blocking or shouting.
- **Do** take a daily picture of the banner.

#### DON'TS

- **Don't** walk in a circle.
- **Don't** block or disrupt pedestrians or vehicles.
- **Don't** place the banner closer than 20 feet from an entrance.
- **Don't** place the banner so that it faces the workplace.
- **Don't** talk to passers-by about the dispute other than to refer them to the union for details.
- **Don't** ask secondary employees to stop working.
- **Don't** take pictures of secondary employees.
- **Don't** try to stop deliveries.
- **Don't** engage in arguments.
- **Don't** use bullhorns or engage in chanting or yelling.
- **Don't** form a gauntlet.

entry or egress. Possible legends: "Labor dispute: Do not patronize,"[165] "Lawbreaker," "Boycott." Smaller letters should advise: "This banner is addressed exclusively to the public and is not intended to cause any employee to refuse to perform services or deliver goods."

Union banners may not say or imply that employees of the secondary employer are on strike. "On Strike for Better Wages" carries this implication.

Unions should accompany bannering with handbills identifying the struck employer and its relationship to the secondary. Handbills should be on hand even if there is little or no foot traffic.

**Numbers.** No more than one or two banners should be used at one location. Forcing persons to walk through a gauntlet is coercive. If two banners are employed, hold them well apart.

**Locations.** Banners should be stationed away from the secondary's entrances and driveways. Messages should face the street.

**Signage laws.** Some cities and towns limit the size of outdoor signs. Check the wording: the ordinance may only be directed at signs attached to buildings or anchored in the ground.

**Holders.** The number of union members present should not exceed the number needed to hold the banner and distribute flyers. Holders should remain in place, although slight foot shuffling is permissible. Clothing can be worn with slogans such as "boycott team."

## Ballooning

Another lawful publicity tactic is to fly a large animal-shaped balloon—a rat, skunk, or pig—in front of the secondary's premises, and to dress handbillers in similar costumes. The NLRB says such "peaceful expressive activity" is a lawful means to disseminate ideas.[166] The fact that passers-by stop to observe or ask questions does not make the activity confrontational.

# Questions and Answers

### Parade

Q. Can we parade through downtown streets with signs condemning a company for doing business with our employer?

A. Yes, if the parade does not stop for an extended period in front of the secondary.[167]

### Charity case

Q. The president of our company serves on the boards of three charities. Can we buy advertisements and distribute flyers asking the public not to donate to these organizations?

A. Yes, if you truthfully explain the reason for the request.

### Bluster

Q. An office products company delivers to our employer on a daily basis. When we handbilled and bannered its headquarters, the supplier sent a letter threatening to sue the union for "tortious interference with business relations." Are we at risk?

A. Not if your materials are truthful. A union can only be held liable for tortious interference during a labor dispute if it makes factual assertions that are deliberately or recklessly false.[168]

## Home sweet home

Q. We are trying to persuade a large customer to suspend business with our employer. Can we picket the home of the customer's president?

A. Hard to say. A divided 1999 Board decision ruled that a union that picketed the home of a secondary official violated Section 8(b)(4).[169] But a 2009 NLRB General Counsel memorandum suggests that secondary picketing must include an attempt to persuade persons not to enter a place of business, an element obviously missing at a residence.[170]

## Student supporters

Q. A student organization has volunteered to picket a customer in our place. Will the union be insulated from legal action?

A. Not necessarily. If the student group is acting as the union's agent, both it and the union can be charged with Section 8(b)(4) violations.[171] To reduce the risk, play no role in the planning, do not pay for signs or leaflets, and instruct your members not to take part.

# 10

## Benefit Daze

*Health insurance* ◆ *Unemployment benefits* ◆
*Vacation pay* ◆ *Disability benefits*

**B**ENEFIT ISSUES AFFECT many strikes. If the employer stops paying for health insurance, workers will be burdened. If strikers are awarded unemployment insurance, pressure will mount on the employer.

### Health insurance

The NLRA allows a struck employer to stop paying for employee health insurance without giving notice to the union or bargaining.[172]

This is not a cause for panic. Strikers may be able to obtain coverage under a spouse's plan. Some union-sponsored health and welfare plans continue coverage during strikes despite a cessation of employer contributions. Some unions maintain a special fund to help strikers pay medical bills. Some strikers may be able to qualify for Medicaid. A final alternative is to elect self-paying status under the federal "COBRA" law.

**COBRA.** The federal COBRA law allows strikers and their families to continue membership in the employer's group health plans for up to eighteen months. The employee, however, must pay the entire premium, including the amount formerly paid by the employer. COBRA applies to workplaces with 20 or more employees. State laws sometimes cover smaller workplaces.

After receiving a stop-payment notice from a struck employer, the group health plan must promptly inform all affected employees of the date coverage ended or will end. The notice must inform the employee of his or her right to become a self-payer under the COBRA law.

Health plans must allow strikers and their beneficiaries 60 calendar days to elect self-paying status from the day the employer stops making payments or the date of the COBRA notice, whichever is later. Following election, the plan must allow employees 45 days to send in the initial premium check. In the interim, the plan must continue coverage. Accordingly, by waiting until the last day to elect COBRA coverage, and by taking full advantage of the grace period, an employee can retain group health coverage for up to 105 days before having to remit a premium. With luck, the strike will conclude before this date and the employer will take responsibility for some or all of the past due premiums.

**Medicaid.** Strikers sometimes qualify for free medical coverage through state Medicaid programs. Income and asset criteria vary widely. The union should research local rules and obtain application forms.

## Unemployment benefits

All states and territories have unemployment insurance (UI) programs. Although most disqualify strikers, there are exceptions.

**New York.** New York disqualifies strikers for seven weeks. The eighth week counts as a waiting period. Benefits are paid in the ninth.

**West Virginia.** West Virginia awards benefits if a strike is triggered by wages, hours, or conditions that are "substantially less favorable" than those of similar workers in the locality.

**Stoppage states.** Eighteen states and Puerto Rico (see list below) limit disqualifications to strikes that cause a "stoppage of work." This is usually considered as a drop in production or operations of 20 to 30 percent. Strikers qualify for UI benefits if the employer maintains or resumes full or close to full operations.

---

### STATES THAT AWARD UI BENEFITS WHEN A STRIKE FAILS TO CAUSE A STOPPAGE OF WORK

Alaska, Delaware, Georgia, Hawaii, Illinois, Iowa, Kansas, Maine, Maryland, Massachusetts, Mississippi, Missouri, Nebraska, New Hampshire, New Jersey, Utah, Vermont, West Virginia

---

**Example:** In the first month of a strike, Reed Corp., a Massachusetts company, experienced an almost complete halt in production. In the second month, supervisors, managers, and white-collar workers increased output to 42 percent of normal. In the third month, output increased to 75 percent, qualifying strikers for UI benefits.[173]

Employers sometimes argue that though they are maintaining full or close to full operations, they are experiencing a stoppage of work because of the effects of a strike on maintenance, research, and other support functions. Such claims have been rejected, one court ruling that: "A stoppage of work requires more than the holes in coverage that inevitably result when staff is temporarily diverted from one place to another."[174]

**Pointer:** Stoppage determinations may hinge on the scope of operations being evaluated. If you are striking all of your employer's facilities, and some are continuing to operate while others are not, ask the UI agency to look at each facility separately. If you are striking one out of many facilities, urge the agency to evaluate the employer's operations as a whole.

**Permanent replacement.** UI programs commonly award benefits if an employer notifies a striker that he or she has been permanently replaced.[175] Some programs award benefits if a business hires a full complement of replacements, even if strikers are not personally notified.

## Vacation pay

An employee who was scheduled for a paid vacation can insist on a cash payout if the scheduled period falls within the strike. If the employer refuses, the union should file a ULP charge.[176]

Employers sometimes argue that a vacation is a break from work and that since strikers are not working they cannot qualify. This argument fails if the employer has a practice of awarding vacation pay during medical, union, or industrial accident leaves, when employees work through their vacation periods, or when employees are terminated. The employer has a stronger argument if the expired contract requires employees to work the day before or the day after a vacation.

## Disability benefits

Workers who are receiving company disability benefits when a strike begins are usually entitled to continued payments, even if the employee takes part in picketing.[177] Strikers who become disabled during a strike are usually ineligible.

The wording of some disability plans allows benefits to be suspended during strikes. For example, the plan may require that the employee be disabled from taking part in "scheduled work." If the facility is no longer operating, scheduled work may not be available.

# Questions and Answers

### Multi-state workforce

Q. Our members live in three states. Which UI program will control—the state where the employee lives or the state where the workplace is located?

A. The state where the workplace is located.

### Food stamps

Q. Can strikers qualify for food stamps?

A. Only if they are pregnant, over age 60, or caring for a child less than six years of age. Employees who are permanently replaced or locked out can also qualify.

### Workers' compensation

Q. Some of our members are on workers' compensation. Does the insurer have to continue their benefits during a strike?

A. Yes, assuming that they remain disabled.

### Holiday pay

Q. If our strike goes through December, will the company have to pay us holiday pay for Christmas as required in the expired contract?

A. Not necessarily. Although the expired contract controls, many agreements require employees to work the day before a holiday, the day after, or both.

### Domino strike

Q. If we strike the shipping department and the company lays everyone else off, will the laid-off workers be awarded unemployment insurance?

A. Probably not. Most UI programs disqualify claimants who are laid off due to a walkout by other members of the union.

### Strike pay

**Q.** If members are successful in applying for UI benefits, will the state reduce their weekly checks by the amount they receive from the union as strike pay?

**A.** This depends on state law. Many states do not regard strike pay as earned income.

### Drop in orders

**Q.** After our six-month strike settled, half of the bargaining unit was unable to return due a steep drop in orders. Should they file for UI?

**A.** Yes. Most states pay UI benefits to strikers who are not recalled when a strike is over.

### End game

**Q.** If the employer closes for good during the strike, will strikers qualify for UI benefits?

**A.** Generally, yes, unless the strike prevented the worker from earning the minimum amount needed to open a claim.

# 11

# Strikebreakers

*Replacements* ◆ *Non-strikers and crossovers* ◆
*Withdrawing recognition*

PERSONS WHO WORK DURING A STRIKE are called strikebreakers. This morally challenged group includes newly hired
replacements, transfers from other facilities, and bargaining
unit members who remain at work or return.

## Replacements

*The National Labor Relations Act (NLRA)* allows employers considerable freedom in hiring workers during strikes and setting their
terms of employment.

**Hiring.** Replacement workers can be hired before or during a strike on either a temporary or a permanent basis. The employer does not have to give the union notice nor explain its reasons. There is one exception: hiring workers on a permanent basis is illegal if the purpose is to damage or destroy the union.[178]

A colorful description of a strikebreaker is thought to have been penned by author Jack London in the early 1900's:

# The Scab

After God had finished the rattlesnake, the toad, and the vampire, He had some awful substance left with which he made a "SCAB."

A SCAB is a two-legged animal with a corkscrew soul, a waterlogged brain, and a combination backbone of jelly and glue. Where others have hearts, he carries a tumor of rotten principles.

When a SCAB comes down the street, men turn their backs, angels weep in heaven, and the devil shuts the gates of hell to keep him out.

No man has a right to SCAB so long as there is a pool of water deep enough to drown his body in, or a rope long enough to hang his carcass with. Judas Iscariot was a gentleman compared with a SCAB. For betraying his master, he had character enough to hang himself. A SCAB has not.

Esau sold his birthright for a mess of pottage. Judas sold his Savior for thirty pieces of silver. Benedict Arnold sold his country for a promise of a commission in the British army. The modern strikebreaker sells his birthright, his country, his wife, his children, and his fellowmen for an unfulfilled promise from his employer, trust, or corporation.

Esau was a traitor to himself. Judas was a traitor to his God. Benedict Arnold was a traitor to his country. A SCAB is a traitor to his God, his country, his family, and his class.

**Example:** During a strike in 2009, a Minnesota factory hired temporary replacements for its entire workforce. A few weeks later the union scheduled a return-to-work vote. Learning about it from a disaffected member, the company hurriedly made the temporaries permanent. When the union submitted its offer to return, the company said that there were no vacancies.

The union filed charges with the NLRB contending that the company made the replacements permanent solely to prevent strikers from returning. An NLRB judge agreed, found an unfair labor practice, and ordered the employer to reinstate strikers with back pay.[179]

**Pay, benefits, and working conditions.** The union does not represent replacement workers while a strike is in progress. Consequently, the employer can set their pay, benefits, and working conditions without regard to the expired contract and without bargaining.[180]

**Requesting information.** Unions have a vital interest in knowing whether a replacement is temporary or permanent. One way to find out is to file an information request. The employer must disclose the name and address of any employee hired on a permanent basis.[181] It must also furnish his or her hire date, position, shift, and wage rate. Data must be provided even if the replacement objects. An employer that denies or ignores a union information request risks converting a strike to ULP status.

The only circumstance that permits an employer to withhold names or addresses is where threats or violence by strikers have created a "clear and present danger" that the union will use the information for purposes of harassment. Name calling and taunting generally do not warrant this level of concern. [182] If threatening incidents have occurred, the union's assurance that it will not use the information to harass anyone must be credited—unless the employer has a valid reason for disbelief.[183]

**Anti-strikebreaker laws.** Laws in some states restrict the hiring of strike replacements. To the dismay of unions, these measures are usually of no effect. A judicial doctrine called "preemption" nullifies state or local laws that conflict with the NLRA. Courts have refused to enforce laws banning the hiring of:

- Permanent replacements (Minnesota)
- Persons who repeatedly offer themselves for employment during strikes (Michigan)

## Non-strikers and crossovers

Employees who decline to join a strike or who return to work before a strike is over continue to be members of the union bargaining unit. Consequently, the employer may not modify their wages or working conditions without giving prior notice to the union and bargaining to impasse.[184] Unilateral changes—for example, increasing the amount of paid leave or requiring work on a holiday—can convert a strike to ULP status.[185]

**Fines.** The union may fine a member who crosses a picket line. If the member refuses to pay, the union can sue in state court. A reasonable fine is wages earned plus a small amount for administrative costs.

The union cannot fine a member who resigns from the union before returning to work. Union rules that forbid resignations immediately before a strike, or while it is in progress, violate the NLRA.[186]

## Withdrawing recognition

An employer that hires permanent replacements or induces substantial numbers of members to desert a strike may attempt to withdraw recognition from the union.

**Recognition.** The NLRB allows an employer to withdraw union recognition if it has objective proof—for example, a petition signed by 50% of the eligible bargaining unit—that the union no longer enjoys majority support. For the first 12 months of a strike, the eligible bargaining unit consists of strikers, non-strikers, and permanent replacements.

**Example:** Local 21 struck on April 1, 2013. All 40 workers in the bargaining unit joined the walkout. Over the next two weeks, the employer hired 40 permanent replacements, increasing the size of the eligible bargaining unit to 80. On April 15, 2013, the replacement workers circulated a petition declaring that they did not want representation by Local 21. All 40 replacements signed. Three days later, the company withdrew recognition on the ground that the union no longer had majority support.

**Note:** A union can challenge the employer by filing ULP charges contending that the employer actively encouraged employees to sign a disavowal petition,[187] that employer ULPs caused disaffection with the union,[188] or that the employer hired more permanent replacements than necessary.

When a strike extends beyond 12 months, the eligible bargaining unit no longer includes strikers who have been permanently replaced.[189] This makes it easier for the employer to withdraw recognition.

**Example:** On May 1, 2013, 40 workers at radio station WRIX went on strike. Over the next 12 months, the station hired 25 permanent replacements. On May 1, 2014, all of the replacements signed a decertification petition. As the eligible unit is now 40 (25 permanent replacements plus 15 unreplaced strikers) the station can withdraw recognition.

**Decertification election.** Another way for an employer to eliminate union rights is to (secretly) encourage strikebreakers to petition for an NLRB decertification election. The NLRB will conduct a secret vote if it receives a petition signed by 30% of the eligible unit. If a majority of the voters fail to vote for union representation, the employer can cease dealing with the union.[190]

If a decertification election is held within 12 months of the onset of a strike, the voting unit will consist of strikers, nonstrikers, and permanent replacements. Strikers who took equivalent employment elsewhere without an intent to return, whose positions were eliminated for legitimate economic reasons, or whom the employer has discharged for serious misconduct cannot vote.

**Pointer:** Strikers who take jobs elsewhere can preserve their right to vote in a decertification election by continuing to picket or by notifying the employer that they intend to return when the strike is over.[191]

When an election is held more than 12 months after a strike begins, strikers who have been permanently replaced are not permitted to vote unless the walkout is an unfair labor practice strike. In that event, permanently replaced strikers may vote and their replacements may not.

# Questions and Answers

### Resignation letters

Q. Can an employer hand out resignation letters to strikers and suggest that they send them to the union?

A. Yes, if the union has told members that they will be fined if they return to work.

### Byrnes Act

Q. Doesn't the *Byrnes Act* outlaw hiring strikebreakers?

A. No. The *Byrnes Act*, a 1936 federal law, prohibits employers from transporting scabs across state lines to use "force or threats" against peaceful union picketing.[192] The law applies to armed goons, not run-of-the-mill strikebreakers.

### Scab lawsuit

Q. After leaving the plant, a replacement worker was hit by a rock and badly injured. Can she sue the union?

A. This depends. In some states, a strikebreaker can sue a union for picket line injuries even if the assailant is unknown. In others, the scab must prove that the union leadership took part in, directed, or encouraged the attack.

**Sleep-over**

Q. The company is allowing scabs to stay in the plant overnight. Legal?

A. Yes, unless the employer is violating a local housing ordinance.

# 12
# Discharges

*Arbitration* ◆ *Pursuing a case at the NLRB* ◆
*Using the grievance process*

I F A STRIKER IS DISCHARGED or refused reinstatement for misbehavior on the picket line, the union can file a ULP charge at
the National Labor Relations Board (NLRB). It can also make
the striker's reinstatement a strike demand.

When negotiating strike settlements, unions often seek an "amnesty
clause" barring strike-related discipline.[193] In return, the employer may
demand protection for workers who crossed the picket line.

## Arbitration

If amnesty is denied, the union should seek an agreement allowing it to take strike discipline cases to arbitration under the contract's just-cause standard.[194] Another way to secure arbitration rights is to make the new contract retroactive to the expiration date of the prior agreement.

Arbitration generally produces better results than litigation at the NLRB:

- Arbitration can be completed in a matter of months; NLRB cases can drag on for years.

- Arbitrators are more likely to overturn discharges for conduct such as making threats, blocking trucks, or throwing objects.[195] As one arbitrator explained, "What may be called just cause in times of industrial peace is not just cause for discipline during a strike."[196]

- Arbitrators often consider an employer's failure to discharge strikers who committed similar or more serious acts as grounds for reversal.[197] NLRB judges do not view the disparate treatment of other strikers as a defense.[198]

- Unlike NLRB judges, arbitrators often give weight to mitigating factors such as lengthy service, a good disciplinary record, and superior work performance.[199] They are also more likely to take account of extenuating circumstances such as provocation and incitement.[200]

- An arbitrator may overturn discipline if the employer failed to interview the employee before imposing discipline.[201] NLRB judges do not apply an equivalent due process standard.

- Employers have limited rights to appeal arbitration awards to the courts. NLRB decisions are subject to more extensive judicial review.

### Pursuing a case at the NLRB

NLRB charges can be filed up to six months after a discharge or a refusal to reinstate. In addition to claiming a violation of the *National Labor Relations Act (NLRA)*, the charge should assert that the employer's conduct converted the walkout to an unfair labor practice strike.[202]

NLRB standards prohibit discharges for strike-related activity unless the employee engaged in "egregious" misconduct.[203] It is illegal to fire a striker for a minor infraction.

**Clear Pine.** In its early years, the NLRB frequently tolerated picket line excesses. While upholding discharges for physical assaults and property damage, it often labeled verbal threats and casual contact as "strike rhetoric" or "animal exuberance."

A 1984 ruling called *Clear Pine Mouldings* reversed course. The case says that an employer can deny reinstatement if the nature of the striker's actions or statements, under the circumstances, would "reasonably tend to coerce or intimidate" non-strikers.[204] This standard applies whether the target is a replacement, crossover, manager, security guard, contractor, or customer.

**Hit list.** Since *Clear Pine*, the Board has sustained discharges upon proof that a striker:

- Threw a rock, bottle, or other object at a person or a vehicle
- Jumped on a car
- Spit on a linecrosser
- Intentionally struck a vehicle with a picket sign, scratched, kicked or rocked it, or beat on a hood
- Committed a physical assault
- Threatened a linecrosser with bodily injury (on or off the picket line)
- Displayed a gun, knife, pipe, or slingshot
- Placed nails or "jackrocks" on a road or driveway
- Used a vehicle to block a doorway or road
- Pursued a person in a high-speed car chase, tailgated, or swerved in front of a vehicle

**Banter and bravado.** Standing alone, picket line rhetoric such as "We know where you live," "We're going to get you," "I'm waiting for you," "We'll fix you," or "I'll whip your ass," is not a lawful ground for discharge.[205] The NLRB usually classifies such remarks as banter or bravado rather than believable threats of physical harm. However, the same remark accompanied by a physical gesture — for example, waving a stick—may be ruled a genuine threat. Moreover, if acts of violence or property damage have occurred, on or off the picket line, the NLRB may conclude that the remark was intended to be taken seriously.

**Profanity and name-calling.** A striker may not be discharged for profanity, rudeness, or obscene gestures—even if the employer has a zero-tolerance harassment policy.[206] An oft-cited NLRB ruling declares that:

> Offensive, vulgar, defamatory or opprobrious remarks uttered during protected activities will not remove activities from the Act's protection unless they are so flagrant, violent, or extreme as to render the individual unfit for further service.[207]

Nonetheless, the NLRB may sustain a discharge if a striker subjects a linecrosser to an unrelenting tirade of sexual or racial slurs. Obscenities directed at a customer may also be deemed sufficient grounds.[208]

**Note:** If union officers or stewards participate in racially offensive conduct toward linecrossers, or if union officers do nothing to deter such conduct by strikers after it is brought to their attention, a court may sustain a civil rights judgement against the union for creating a "hostile work environment."[209]

**Blocking vehicles.** Strikers have a right to approach vehicles, attempt to talk with drivers, and hand out union literature. Short blockages or minor traffic delays do not warrant discipline.[210]

**Minor arrests.** Ordinarily, an arrest or conviction for trespass, disorderly conduct, or scuffling with police is not grounds for discharge under the NLRA unless evidence establishes that the event had a coercive impact on linecrossers.[211]

**Balancing.** Historically, the NLRB has been more tolerant of misconduct by unfair labor practice strikers than economic strikers. This is known as the *"Thayer* balancing doctrine."[212] Few decisions have applied the doctrine in recent years.

**Grounds for reversal.** Proof of one or more of the following contentions can provide sufficient grounds for the NLRB to overturn a discharge:

- The employer discharged the striker on impulse or speculation without concrete evidence of misconduct.
- The striker did not take part in the acts for which the employer imposed discharge.
- If the striker committed misconduct, it was not serious.
- The employer took action because the striker is a picket captain, union officer, or rank-and-file leader.
- The employer applied double standards (see below).

**Double standards.** An employer may not levy a significantly harsher punishment on a striker than it imposed on a strike replacement, guard, supervisor, or other non-striker who committed similar or more serious misconduct. As one NLRB ruling explained:

> [An employer] may not knowingly tolerate behavior by non-strikers or replacements that is at least as serious as, or more serious than, [the] conduct of strikers that the employer is relying on to deny reinstatement to jobs.[213]

To lay a basis for claims of disparate treatment, the union should keep a log of threats and assaults by supervisors, guards, replacements, and non-strikers. The log should include dates, times, and names of witnesses. Moreover, because the double standards argument is only viable if management was aware of the conduct, the union should send a report to the employer (see below).

---

**INCIDENT REPORT**

**Date:** January 5, 2014
**To:** Tom Smooty, Manager, East Plant
**From:** Marcia Dostal, President, Local 80
**Re:** Assault

This is to inform you that yesterday, January 4, 2014, at the East Gate, supervisor Rick Smith assaulted striker Timothy Wolf by deliberately driving his car toward Wolf and swerving at the last instant.

---

## Using the grievance process

Although arbitration is not compulsory, the union should file grievances against strike discharges and other discipline. As the just cause standard remains in effect, management must meet with the union, discuss the matter, and furnish information.[214] Refusals can convert a strike to ULP status—even if the employee is clearly at fault.[215]

A union information request can demand copies of incident reports, investigative records, logbooks, witness statements, videotapes, personnel files, and other relevant materials. To investigate disparate treatment, records can also be sought concerning misconduct by non-strikers, guards, supervisors, replacements, and other strikers.[216]

# Questions and Answers

### Delayed discipline

Q. Two strikers threw rocks at a company truck. Although they were in plain view, the company did not say anything or take action at the time. However, when the strike ended, it refused to take the employees back to work. If we file charges at the NLRB or go to arbitration, can we argue that the company's failure to act when it observed the misconduct affects its right to take action later?

A. Yes. Long delays in announcing discipline violate due process and suggest that the employer did not view the incidents as serious.[217]

### Search for work

Q. If the NLRB orders an employer to reinstate a striker, will it order back wages?

A. Yes. But it may allow the employer to take a substantial deduction if the striker did not look for work or waited to do so for an unreasonably long period.[218]

### Failure to investigate non-striker

Q. During a hearing at the NLRB, evidence was received that the employer failed to punish a non-striker for serious picket line misconduct. The employer claimed that at the time it did not believe the allegations against the non-striker. Does this get the employer off the hook?

A. Not necessarily. If the employer's investigation of the non-striker was perfunctory—for example, if the employer failed to interview witnesses or review video recordings—the Board may find disparate treatment.[219]

### Timing a ULP charge

Q. We filed an NLRB charge after management discharged a striker. We also asked for a copy of the employer's investigative file. The company says it does not have to answer the information request because of the NLRB charge. What gives?

A. An employer can deny an information request that is submitted to support a pending unfair labor practice charge.[220] It is often better to delay filing a discrimination charge at the NLRB until after the union has submitted a request for information.

# 13
# Name that Strike

*Definitions* ◆ *Reinstatement rights* ◆
*ULP strategy* ◆ *Reconversion*

**M**OST STRIKES END WITH A SETTLEMENT and a new contract. But if the employer stubbornly refuses a reasonable resolution, the union may eventually decide that its best play is to return to work without a contract. The move may be part of a "Trojan horse" strategy to move the struggle inside (see next chapter) or simply an attempt to stop the bleeding. In either case, the rights of strikers to return to their positions may turn on whether the walkout is an economic or an unfair labor practice (ULP) strike.

If no permanent replacements were hired during the walkout, the distinction between an economic and a ULP strike has little significance. Upon receiving the union's unconditional offer to return, the employer must allow all strikers to return to their original positions (with the exception of those who were legitimately discharged or laid off).

A strike's classification becomes critical, however, when the following events transpire:

1. The employer hires permanent replacements, and
2. The union offers to return without conditions, and
3. The employer refuses to dismiss the replacements to make room for strikers.

## Definitions

The classifications "economic" and "unfair labor practice" strike are based on the issues that triggered the work stoppage or prolonged its continuation.

A strike to cause movement in collective bargaining or to oppose an employer's lawful implementation of a final offer is an economic strike. The strike does not have concern economic issues.

A strike caused or prolonged by an employer violation of the *National Labor Relations Act (NLRA)* is an unfair labor practice strike. The violation need not be flagrant. Nor must it be the sole or even the major cause of the walkout. If one of the reasons employees stop work is to protest an unfair labor practice, the walkout is a ULP strike.[221]

A strike that begins as an economic strike can convert to an unfair labor practice strike if the employer commits a ULP violation that causes widespread anger, interferes with bargaining, or strengthens workers' resolve to stay out.[222]

## Reinstatement rights

When a union makes an unconditional offer to return from an economic strike, the employer has two lawful options: accept the offer or declare a lockout.

If the employer accepts the offer, it must immediately allow some or all strikers to return to their original positions. It may reject strikers whose positions are occupied by persons hired as permanent replacements. It may also reject strikers whose jobs have been eliminated because of legitimate business reasons.[223] Strikers whose positions are unavailable must be placed on a preferential recall list (called a Laidlaw list).

When a union makes an unconditional offer to return from an unfair labor practice strike, the employer is legally obligated to allow strikers to return to their former positions even if a permanent replacement must be discharged to create an opening. If the employer refuses, the union can seek reinstatement and back pay at the NLRB.

**Example:** When BK Plastics imposed its final offer before reaching a valid impasse, 100 workers went on a ULP strike. Over the next month, the company hired 60 permanent replacements. To move the situation forward, the union submitted an unconditional back-to-work offer. Disputing the strike's ULP status, the company only recalled 40 strikers. The union promptly filed a ULP charge at the NLRB seeking an order reinstating the 60 unrecalled strikers with back pay from the date it offered to return.

When a union offers to return from a converted ULP strike, the rights of strikers to displace permanent replacements depend on the date the strike changed character. Strikers whose positions were filled by permanent replacements before conversion can be placed on a recall list. Strikers whose positions were filled after conversion are entitled to immediate reinstatement.

**Note:** In some circumstances, an employer can "reconvert" a ULP strike to economic status (see page 140). Permanent replacements hired after reconversion can be retained at the expense of strikers.

---

### LABOR LAW REFORM:
### A BAN ON PERMANENT REPLACEMENTS

Labor unions have long sought to annul the U.S. Supreme Court's 1938 *Mackay Radio* ruling permitting employers to hire permanent replacements during economic strikes. They argue that it contradicts the NLRA's implicit assurance that workers can strike without fear of losing their jobs. In 1992 a bill to overrule *Mackay* sailed through the U.S. House of Representatives only to fall by three votes in the Senate. In 1995 labor persuaded President Bill Clinton to issue an executive order barring federal contracts with employers that permanently replace striking workers. A federal court declared the order unenforceable. Many activists believe that overturning *Mackay* should remain labor's number one legislative priority.

---

## ULP strategy

A union can reduce employee anxiety, block the employer from hiring permanent replacements, and alleviate the risk of decertification by pursuing a ULP strike strategy. A ULP strategy has two components:

1. Identify—or, if necessary, provoke—employer unfair labor practices.
2. Position the strike around a ULP.

**Pre-strike ULPs.** The most common pre-strike ULPs are:

- Bad-faith bargaining
- Refusal to supply relevant information
- Insistence on permissive bargaining subjects
- Unilateral changes
- Threats or discipline against union activists

***Bad-faith bargaining.*** Actions or statements that suggest that the employer intends to avoid a contract are evidence of bad-faith bargaining. Examples include repeatedly cancelling meetings, withholding authority from negotiators, failing to consider compromises, and withdrawing from a tentative agreement without a rational explanation.

Although unions frequently allege that employers are guilty of bad-faith bargaining, the NLRB rarely agrees, often labeling outrageous employer conduct simply as "hard bargaining."

***Refusal to furnish relevant information.*** An employer violates the NLRA if it refuses to furnish documents or data requested by the union to prepare for bargaining or to respond to arguments. A wide range of information must be provided (sometimes contingent on the union signing a confidentiality agreement).

If the employer claims that labor costs are lower in other branches or divisions, ask for the benefit plans and collective-bargaining agreements covering these entities and a breakdown of comparative costs.[224]

If the employer asserts that it is "losing money" or "cannot afford" union demands, request a comprehensive financial audit, including profit-and-loss reports.[225]

If the employer claims that it needs concessions to avoid losing business, ask for a list of customers so that the union can ask them if they are contemplating a change.[226]

If the employer claims that it needs to keep costs from rising, ask whether it has awarded raises or benefit increases to any non-bargaining unit employees including managers, and, if so, the amounts.[227]

***Insistence on a permissive bargaining subject.*** The NLRB classifies bargaining subjects as mandatory, permissive, or illegal. Mandatory subjects relate directly to wages, benefits, or working conditions. Permissive subjects encompass all other lawful matters.

Although an employer may propose language on a permissive

subject, it cannot insist on the proposal as a condition for bargaining or signing an agreement.[228] Declaring impasse on a final offer is a ULP if the offer includes a permissive subject.[229]

Permissive subjects include demands that the union:

- Change the scope or composition of the bargaining unit.
- Reduce dues or initiation fees.
- Give up the right to handbill on nonworking time in nonworking areas.
- Give up rights that accrued under the expired contract.
- Change its contract ratification or strike vote procedures
- Allow the employer to resolve grievances outside the presence of the union.
- Restrict activities outside the employment relationship.
- Agree not to strike after the contract expires.
- Withdraw or settle a ULP charge or lawsuit.
- Accept a government mediator.
- Allow the employer to negotiate directly with individual employees.
- Permit strikers' lawful reinstatement rights to be limited or delayed.
- Agree that strike replacements and non-strikers will have super-seniority.
- Forfeit the reinstatement rights of illegally fired employees.
- Forego discipline of a member who crossed the picket line.

**Unilateral change.** An employer commits a ULP if it makes a significant change in a term or condition of employment without first notifying the union of its intentions and, if the union requests, bargaining the change to impasse or agreement. Implementing a final offer before reaching a bona fide impasse on the entire contract is a common basis for an unfair labor practice strike.[230]

***Threats.*** Threats, surveillance, or discipline directed at union leaders or activists can create a basis for a ULP strike.[231] Job protests can trigger such activities, as even the most sophisticated manager may be unable to exercise restraint when faced with picket lines, rallies, and other contract campaign activities.

**Mid-strike ULPs.** A strike that is economic at its inception converts to ULP status if the employer commits an NLRA violation that prolongs the conflict. Mid-strike ULPs include:

- Refusing to meet with the union
- Discharging strikers without adequate grounds
- Threatening strikers with permanent job losses
- Causing strikers to be wrongly arrested
- Refusing to discuss grievances
- Violence or threats of violence by employer agents
- Videotaping peaceful picketing or rallies
- Bribing employees to return
- Refusing to pay accrued benefits
- Granting superseniority to non-strikers or replacements
- Unilaterally changing the terms of employment of non-strikers
- Bypassing union representatives to deal directly with unit employees

For other examples, see pages 56–58.

**Positioning a ULP strike.** Filing a meritorious charge at the NLRB does not guarantee a strike ULP status. The union must also convince the agency that the ULP played a significant role in the union's decision to strike or to stay out. The union can help its case by taking the following measures.

**Inform the membership.** The mindset of members is crucial. If union leaders are the only ones aware of the employer's illegal conduct, the strike is unlikely to win ULP certification.

Before holding a membership strike vote, the union should fully explain the ULP violation and enter the discussion into the minutes. The ballot should refer to the ULP. Example:

> Do the members agree to strike because the employer has violated the National Labor Relations Act by making unilateral changes in our terms and conditions of employment and because it has refused to negotiate a fair collective bargaining agreement?

If the strike begins as an economic strike, but the employer commits a ULP that impedes bargaining or angers the workforce, the union should take a vote to continue the walkout as a ULP strike. The ballot may be phrased as follows:

> Do the members agree that in view of the employer's unfair labor practice, namely _____, they shall continue the strike?

**Inform the employer.** The union should notify the employer that it considers its walkout to be a ULP strike. Letters and emails to the employer should refer to the infractions. A remedy for the ULP should be included in the union's bargaining demands and raised repeatedly.

**Inform the press and the public.** Press releases and letters should be sent to newspapers, politicians, and clergy describing the walkout as

an unfair labor practice strike. Union officials should emphasize the point during press interviews. Picket signs should cite the ULP. Examples: "On strike against bad faith bargaining," "On strike because of unilateral changes."

*Push the NLRB.* When a union files a ULP charge during a strike, it should claim that the violation caused or is prolonging the work stoppage. If a charge predated the strike, submit an amendment asserting that the ULP triggered the walkout. The NLRB Case-handling Manual instructs regional offices to investigate connections between ULPs and strikes and, when appropriate, to include a ULP-strike allegation when issuing a complaint.[232]

---

### ULP CHARGE

1. On August 1, 2014, the employer videotaped peaceful union picketing.

2. On August 4, 2014, a supervisor threatened a striker that the plant would close.

3. On August 6, 2014, a supervisor purposely drove into the picket line.

The above actions violate the NLRA and have caused or prolonged the strike currently engaged in by the bargaining unit.

---

## Reconversion

As if the law was not already confusing, the NLRB allows an employer to "reconvert" a ULP strike to economic status by "fully remedying" the misconduct that caused or prolonged the walkout. Permanent replacements hired after reconversion can displace strikers.

To qualify for reconversion, an employer must:

- Admit wrongdoing and repudiate the illegal conduct.
- Publicize the repudiation to the bargaining unit.
- Make employees whole for any losses caused by the violation.
- Assure employees that it will not commit other NLRA violations.[233]

---

### A UNION OFFICER IS NOT A POTTED PLANT

A union may take deliberate steps to position a walkout as a ULP strike. Responding to an employer who argued that preparation tainted a union's claim, an NLRB judge declared:

> It is uncontroverted that the employees at the May 13 meeting freely and unanimously voted, by secret ballot, to engage in a ULP strike. There is no evidence whatsoever that the employees were threatened or otherwise coerced by [union president] Cahill or other union officials. Nevertheless, the [employer argues] that an adverse inference should be drawn from the fact that Cahill and [union attorney] Lohman advised the employees on whether to engage in a ULP or economic strike, educated them about the rules for engaging in a ULP strike, and provided assistance to them so that they followed the rules and did not lose their jobs. Such an argument must obviously fail; to hold otherwise would require employee representatives to be nothing but potted plants.[234]

---

# Questions and Answers

### Kick in the butt

Q. The company's chief negotiator announced that due to its hiring of permanent replacements, the company was withdrawing its agreement to a union security clause. Does this convert our strike to ULP status?

A. No. An employer can alter its bargaining position, withdraw from tentative agreements, and demand new concessions during a strike.

### Can replacements sue?

Q. We are trying to settle our strike but the hospital will not discharge the permanent replacements. The HR Director claims they could sue the company for breach of contract. Is she blowing smoke?

A. Hard to say. As a rule, an employer can fire a replacement worker for any reason. The rule does not apply, however, if the employer expressly promised a replacement that she will keep her job despite a settlement with the union. To evaluate the employer's concern, request all contracts or correspondence between the company and the replacements.

> **Pointer:** Because a proposal to fire permanent replacements is a permissive subject of bargaining, the union should not insist on the demand as a condition of settling the strike.

### OSHA violation

Q. Is a strike that is triggered by a company OSHA violation a ULP strike?

A. No. Violations of laws other than the NLRA, such as the OSH Act, the FLSA, Title VII, or ERISA, do not create a lawful basis for a ULP strike.

### Mistaken belief

Q. After filing three unfair labor practice charges, we went on strike under the genuine belief that the employer had engaged in bad faith bargaining and other NLRA violations. If the NLRB decides against us on all of the charges, will our strike still be an unfair labor practice strike?

A. No. An honest or well-reasoned belief that the employer committed unfair labor practices is not sufficient. If the Board concludes that the employer's actions were lawful, the strike is only an economic strike.

# 14

# Offer to Return

*Trojan horse strategy* ◆ *After-the-fact offer*

CRUNCH TIME. If a struck employer begins to hire permanent replacements, the union must rapidly assess its position. If the number is small, the union may be able to shrug the move off as a scare tactic. But if the employer appears intent on hiring a significant complement, the strike, and indeed the union's very existence, may be in jeopardy. In these circumstances, the union's options are:

• Continue the strike.

• Make the best deal possible, even if it means giving in to the employer's demands.

- Return to work without a contract.

Continuing the strike is high risk. An employer that hires permanent replacements is likely to insist on union busting concessions such as ending seniority, dues checkoff, and union security. It may even try to withdraw recognition or petition for a decertification election. Unless the union is extremely confident that its walkout will qualify as an unfair labor practice strike, it should consider other strategies.

Signing an agreement on the employer's terms may be too hard to swallow. What about returning to work without a contract?

## Trojan horse strategy

A union that offers to return to work without a contract can derail an employer plan to replace the workforce. Under the *National Labor Relations Act (NLRA)*, when a union submits an unconditional offer to return from a strike, the employer has two choices: reinstate strikers immediately (other than economic strikers whose jobs are occupied by permanent replacements) or declare a lockout. In either case the employer may not hire additional permanent replacements.[235]

**The struggle continues.** A union that returns without a contract can pursue its campaign from the inside.[236] Workers may wear insignia, hold rallies, conduct informational picketing, urge customers to boycott, and engage in other pressure tactics (see Chapter 2). The employer must continue to bargain over a new agreement. If the union fails to achieve an acceptable agreement, it can walk out again. A "Trojan horse" campaign may be more effective than the strike it replaces.

**Note:** The absence of a contract does not enable the employer to make unilateral changes in the wages, benefits, or working conditions of returning workers. As explained in Chapter 2, except for union shop and arbitration procedures, an employer must continue to follow the terms and conditions of the expired contract including dues checkoff and past practices. Changes may only be made if bargaining reaches a valid impasse on the entire agreement.

**Formulating the offer.** A return-to-work offer should be in writing. Email is acceptable. The offer may not include any conditions

or qualifications, for example, a demand that the employer reinstate a discharged striker.

---

**RETURN-TO-WORK OFFER**

**Date:** December 10, 2014
**To:** Walter Hamilton, President, Northeast Utilities Co.
**From:** Nora Breakstone, President, Local 20
**Re:** Return to work without conditions

This is to notify the company that Local 20 offers to end the strike and return to work immediately without conditions. We make this offer for all employees represented by Local 20 and all employees who have honored the picket line.

If the number of returning strikers exceeds the number of available positions, the union requests a meeting to discuss the procedure for filling vacancies.

Please notify the union when workers can report to work.

---

**Pointer:** Keep the union's intention to return to work under wraps until the offer is submitted. Otherwise, the employer may accelerate the hiring of permanent replacements.

**Request for information.** Soon after making an offer to return, the union should request an up-to-date list of the names and addresses of any permanent replacements along with their hiring letters and employment agreements. A request should also be submitted for the names of any subcontractors doing bargaining unit work, the nature and extent of such services, and copies of contracts.[237]

**Reinstatement.** Unless it declares a lockout, an employer that receives an unconditional return-to-work offer must put eligible strikers back to work immediately. Delay requires a substantial business justification.[238] Preconditions, such as job applications, interviews, or the withdrawal of NLRB charges, may not be imposed.[239] Strikers must be restored to their pre-strike positions or to jobs with equivalent salaries and duties. Strikers for whom positions are unavailable must be placed on a preferential recall list.

> **Note:** Unless bargained with the employer, a returning striker cannot bump a crossover or non-striker, even if the striker has greater seniority.[240]

**Challenging permanent replacements.** A returning union can challenge the retention of a permanent replacement by filing a ULP charge contending that the employer did not hire the replacement on a permanent basis. To qualify a replacement as permanent, the employer and the employee must have had a mutual understanding, at the time of hire or later, that the job would continue beyond the strike.[241] Applications, personnel files, or correspondence may reveal that the employer told a replacement that a final decision would not be made until the end of the strike.

> **Note:** Unions sometime argue that a replacement hired on an "at will" basis, or subject to a probationary period, cannot be classified as permanent. The Board does not agree.[242]

**Recall list.** An employer that accepts a return-to-work offer must place unreinstated strikers on a preferential recall list. The following rules apply:

- The employer must bargain with the union over how to order the list. The usual method is departmental or plant seniority.

The employer may only impose a different method—for example, arranging workers in order of merit—if it bargains the method to impasse and the method does not discriminate against union leaders or activists.

- In the event of a vacancy or the creation of a new position, the employer must contact all employees on the list who are qualified to perform the job.
- A striker who is offered a job significantly different from the striker's pre-strike position can decline without losing his or her position on the list. If the striker accepts, and the striker's pre-strike position or its equivalent opens up in the future, the employer must allow a transfer.
- The list must be maintained until all strikers have been offered employment.

### After-the-fact offer

The return-to-work offer described above is designed for submission soon after the union learns that the employer is hiring permanent replacements.

If the union misses this opportunity, and the employer hires a large complement of permanent replacements, the union should consider making an "after-the-fact" offer. The efficacy of such an offer depends on the union having positioned its walkout as a ULP strike. In these circumstances, an after-the-fact offer can enable strikers to qualify for unemployment insurance benefits and provide a basis for an NLRB order reinstating strikers with back pay.

```
┌─────────────────────────────────────────────────────────┐
│              AFTER-THE-FACT OFFER                        │
│                                                          │
│  Date: December 10, 2014                                 │
│  To: Walter Hamilton, President, Northeast Utilities     │
│  From: Nora Breakstone, President, Local 20              │
│  Re: Return to work                                      │
│  On November 1, 2014, Local 20 commenced an unfair labor │
│  practice strike against Northeast Utilities. This letter│
│  is to notify Northeast Utilities that the union is      │
│  unconditionally offering to end the strike and          │
│  immediately return to work. Local 20 makes this offer on│
│  behalf of all employees in the bargaining unit and all  │
│  employees who are honoring the picket line.             │
└─────────────────────────────────────────────────────────┘
```

**NLRB charges.** When a union submits an unconditional offer to return from a ULP strike, the law requires the employer to reinstate all eligible employees within five days—even if this requires it to dismiss some or all of its permanent replacements. If, as is likely, the employer refuses, the union can file NLRB charges seeking reinstatement and back pay.

**Example:** On June 2, 125 Trixie employees went on strike to protest the discharge of the union president. Over the next two months, Trixie hired 120 permanent replacements. On August 1, asserting that the walkout was a ULP strike, the union submitted an unconditional offer to return. Trixie responded that the strike was economic and that only six positions were open.

Disputing the employer, the union filed an NLRB charge contending that all 125 strikers should have been reinstated.[243] It also instructed its members to file for unemployment insurance benefits on the ground that the employer has replaced them or locked them out. Picketing continued.

**Back-pay clock.** An offer to return starts the back-pay clock for each eligible ULP striker not offered reinstatement. The clock keeps ticking until the employee is allowed to return. This can give the union considerable leverage. For example, if 100 strikers have average weekly wages of $800, the employer's potential back-pay liability will grow by more than $80,000 per week.[244]

**Unemployment insurance.** In most states, a striker whose request to return is denied qualifies for unemployment insurance benefits.[245] Payouts will be charged to the employer, increasing its incentive to settle.

# Questions and Answers

### Reconnaissance

Q. We are thinking of sending a union member into the plant for a few days to check on wages and working conditions. If the member submits an unconditional offer to return, does the company have to allow her back?

A. Yes, if her position or an equivalent is available.[246]

### Group request

Q. Can an employer ignore a union return-to-work offer on the ground that each striker must make an individual request?

A. No. The union speaks for its members.

# 15

# Lockouts

*Lawful and unlawful • UI benefits*

ITHHOLDING EMPLOYMENT from otherwise willing employees is termed a lockout. The tactic is often used by employers to gain leverage in labor disputes. Even as the number of strikes in the U.S. has dropped, the number of lockouts has increased dramatically.

Unions have long feared lockouts. In recent years, however, some have perceived a silver (or perhaps a silver-plated) lining. When a union and an employer are heading toward a pitched battle, a lockout has several advantages over a strike:

- In most states, employees can qualify for unemployment benefits (taxable to the employer).
- The employer cannot hire permanent replacements.
- The public and the press are more supportive.
- If the employer commits an unfair labor practice that affects negotiations, the NLRB can declare the lockout unlawful, order employees reinstated, and award back pay.

Although an employer is allowed to operate during a lockout, the union can picket, attempt to shut the employer down, and organize boycotts against customers, suppliers, and other influential secondaries (see Chapter 9). The union can also unleash a punishing corporate campaign (see page 60).

## Lawful and unlawful

For many years the law only allowed lockouts for defensive reasons, for example, to avoid a surprise strike or sabotage. But in a 1965 decision known as *American Ship*, the U.S. Supreme Court changed course, ruling that an employer could declare a lockout to force a union to accept a contract.[247]

*American Ship* set one important condition, however, stating that an employer can only undertake an offensive lockout if its bargaining position is "legitimate." [248] If one or more ULPs significantly taint the employer's position, the NLRB can rule the lockout unlawful, require the employer to call employees back, and order the payment of full back wages.

Infractions that can make a lockout unlawful include:
- Bad-faith bargaining
- Insistence on a permissive subject
- Imposition of a final offer before reaching a good-faith impasse
- Failure to announce the precise terms on which the union must agree to end the lockout
- Hiring permanent replacements
- Inviting anti-union workers to remain on the job
- Any other ULPs, including illegal discharges, that delay resolution of the underlying labor dispute

**Bad-faith bargaining.** A lockout may be ruled unlawful if the employer refuses to bargain on a new agreement, maintains a rigid take-it-or-leave-it attitude, insists on demands that deny the union its representational rights, withdraws tentative agreements without good cause, deliberately misleads the union, submits proposals designed to frustrate the bargaining process, refuses to provide relevant information, or commits other bargaining violations.

**Permissive subject.** A lockout to force agreement on a permissive subject of bargaining is unlawful.[249] Permissive subjects include demands that the union withdraw a ULP charge, drop a lawsuit, or change the scope of the bargaining unit. It is immaterial that all other demands are mandatory subjects.

**Final offer.** A lockout to force a union to accept a final offer is unlawful if the employer implemented the offer before reaching a bona fide bargaining impasse.[250]

**Conditions for return.** A lockout is unlawful if the employer fails to promptly announce the terms with which the union must agree to bring the lockout to an end.[251] The terms must be clear: demanding that the union sign a contract is inadequate if the terms are confusing or a "moving target."[252]

**Permanent replacements.** Hiring permanent replacements during a lockout makes the lockout illegal. As an NLRB ruling states: "An employer's use of permanent replacements is inconsistent with a declared lawful lockout in support of its bargaining position."[253]

> **Pointer:** To learn whether the employer is hiring replacements on a permanent basis, submit a request for copies of contracts with new employees as well as correspondence and emails.

**Selective lockout.** An employer can allow a bargaining unit member to work during a lockout if its invitation is based on a legitimate need. For example, an employer can ask an employee with a unique skill set to stay on.[254]

A lockout is illegal, however, if the employer asks employees to work because they are not members of the union or have not taken part in union activities. An employer that declares a lockout when a union offers to return from a strike cannot invite non-strikers and crossovers to work.[255] The Board has not decided the legality of retaining permanent replacements who were hired during a strike.

## UI benefits

Thirty-eight states award unemployment insurance (UI) to employees who are locked out. Eligibility criteria vary. Seven states (Alaska, Delaware, Georgia, Hawaii, Missouri, and Nebraska) pay benefits only if the employer maintains full or close to full operations. California distinguishes between offensive lockouts (benefits awarded) and defensive lockouts (benefits denied). Massachusetts does not award benefits if an employer declares a lockout in response to substantial and repeated property damage or if employees are unwilling to work under the terms of an expired labor agreement. Indiana disqualifies claimants if bargaining is at an impasse. Wisconsin and New Jersey withhold payments if the lockout comes on the heels of a strike.

---

### STATES THAT AWARD UI
### BENEFITS DURING LOCKOUTS

Alaska, Arkansas, California, Colorado, Connecticut, Delaware, Florida, Georgia, Hawaii, Illinois, Indiana, Iowa, Kentucky, Louisiana, Maine, Maryland, Massachusetts, Minnesota, Mississippi, Missouri, Montana, Nebraska, New Hampshire, New Jersey, New York, Ohio, Oklahoma, Oregon, Pennsylvania, Rhode Island, South Dakota, Texas, Tennessee, Utah, Vermont, Washington, West Virginia, Wisconsin

---

# Questions and Answers

**Scare tactic**

Q. Our contract expires tomorrow. The company says that unless the union signs a new agreement, it will declare a lockout. Isn't this bad-faith bargaining?

A. No. An employer can threaten a lockout to pressure a union to accept its demands.

**WARN**

Q. The federal WARN law says employers must give 60 days advance notice before a closure or mass layoff. Does this law apply to lockouts?

## A. No.[256]

### Permanent outsourcing

**Q.** Can an employer permanently farm out work during a lockout?

**A.** The authorities are in conflict. The NLRB says that permanently subcontracting bargaining unit work during a lockout is unlawful because it is more harmful to employee rights than hiring permanent replacements.[257] The D.C. Court of Appeals disagrees.[258]

### Unlawful to lawful

**Q.** We told the employer that its lockout is illegal because one of its demands is that the union drop a class-action lawsuit. If the employer withdraws this proposal, does the lockout become lawful?

**A.** No. The only way to "cure" an unlawful lockout is to reinstate workers and reimburse them for lost wages.[259]

### Health insurance

**Q.** Can a company stop paying for health insurance during a lockout?

**A.** Not unless it gives notice to the union and permits meaningful bargaining.[260]

### Sympathy strikers

**Q.** If an office worker honors our picket line during a lockout, could the employer permanently replace her?

**A.** No. Sympathy strikers have the same rights as the employees they support. Locked out workers cannot be permanently replaced.

### UI requirements

Q. Do employees who receive unemployment insurance during a lockout have to look for work each week?

A. Yes.

### Multi-employer lockout

Q. Our company has an agreement with three of its competitors that if one is struck, the others will declare lockouts. Lawful?

A. Yes.

### Financial information

Q. The company is refusing our request to inspect their financial records despite their claim that they are unable to pay more than their final offer. Does this taint their lockout?

A. Yes. A refusal to supply information needed by a union to evaluate an employer's claims can make a lockout unlawful.[261]

# Glossary

**Ally** Business that is closely integrated with the struck employer or is performing struck work.

**Ambulatory picketing** Picketing directed at scabs working on a secondary site.

**Administrative Law Judge (ALJ)** Presides over NLRB hearings and issues recommended decisions.

**Board** Five-person NLRB panel that reviews ALJ decisions.

**Circuit court** Federal court with power to affirm or vacate Board decisions.

**Conversion** Transformation of economic strike to ULP strike.

**Economic strike** Strike for union recognition or to obtain movement in collective bargaining.

**FMCS** Federal Mediation and Conciliation Service.

**Impasse** Point in negotiations where neither party is willing to make concessions and further bargaining appears to be futile.

**Informational picketing** Picketing to advertise a labor dispute without attempting to stop employees from working

**Intermittent strike** Repeated walkouts designed to confuse and unsettle an employer.

**Lockout** Prohibiting some or all bargaining unit employees from working in order to gain an advantage in collective bargaining or to defend against an imminent protest.

**Mandatory bargaining subject** Matter directly relating to a term or condition of employment.

**NLRA** National Labor Relations Act.

**NLRB** National Labor Relations Board.

**Partial strike** Refusal to perform an assigned or expected duty.

**Permissive bargaining subject** Matter that indirectly affects employees, involves internal union affairs, or lies within traditional managerial prerogatives.

**Reserved gate** Entrance reserved for struck employer, its employees, agents, and suppliers.

**Scab** Employee who works during a strike.

**Secondary employee** Person employed by a secondary employer.

**Secondary employer (also called a "neutral" employer)** Employer other than struck employer or its allies.

**Secondary picketing** Picketing employer with whom the union does not have a direct dispute.

**Section 8(b)(4)** Section of NLRA forbidding secondary picketing and other coercive activities directed against secondary employers.

**Slowdown** Deliberate reduction in employee efforts.

**Sympathy strike** Refusal to cross union picket line.

**Unfair labor practice (ULP)** Violation of NLRA by employer or union.

**Unfair labor practice strike (ULP strike)** Strike caused, in whole or in part, by employer NLRA violations.

**Unilateral change** Change in mandatory subject of bargaining without prior notice to the union or adequate opportunity to bargain.

# Notes

The endnotes cite National Labor Relations Board (NLRB) and court decisions. It is often helpful to refer to legal decisions when filing ULP charges or meeting with NLRB investigators.

NLRB decisions are published in a reporter called *Decisions and Orders of the National Labor Relations Board*, abbreviated as NLRB. There are currently 359 volumes.

The citation, International Paper Co., 319 NLRB 1253, 1266 (1995), refers to a decision that appears in volume 319 of the NLRB reporter beginning on page 1253. Page 1266 is where the matter at issue is discussed or where a quotation originates. The decision was issued in 1995. It takes approximately three years for the NLRB to paginate a decision. Thus, the citation Fleet Drugs, 357 NLRB No. 20, slip op. at 9 (2011), refers to page 9 of the "slip opinion."

NLRB decisions are available on the NLRB website: www.nlrb.gov. Click Cases and Decisions, Case Decisions, and Board Decisions. Enter the proper volume number. Then scroll down the alphabetical list of case names. You can also enter the volume and page (i.e., 319 NLRB 1253) into Google search which will often take you to the case.

Federal circuit court decisions are cited as: Culinary Workers Local 226 v. NLRB, 309 F.3d 578, 582 (9th Cir. 2002). The decision is found in volume 309 of a reporter called Federal Reporter Third Series, beginning on page 578. It was issued by the Ninth Circuit in 2002.

U.S. Supreme Court citations are cited as: NLRB v. Truitt Mfg. Co., 351 U.S. 149, 153 (U.S. Sup. Ct. 1956). The decision is in volume 351 of a reporter called U.S. Reports. It begins on page 149. The most relevant page is 153.

Court decisions can often be found using Google.

**Note:** For space and simplicity, NLRB citations in the endnotes do not include appeals to the U.S. Circuit Courts or the U.S. Supreme Court. Such histories should be listed when citing decisions in a legal brief.

1  *See* Palm Court Nursing Home, 341 NLRB 813, 819 (2004) ("Long-standing precedent establishes that employers and unions have the right to choose whomever they wish to represent them in formal labor negotiations."); Caribe Staple Co., 313 NLRB 877, 889 (1994) (employer cannot insist that union reduce size of bargaining team); Standard Oil Co. of Ohio, 137 NLRB 690, 690 (1962) (employer may not condition bargaining on union not including temporary bargaining team members). **But note:** If the employer is paying wages for bargaining time, the union may not have a right to unilaterally enlarge the size of its bargaining team.

2   *See* Bartlett-Collins Co., 237 NLRB 770, 773 (1978) (threshold matters, preliminary and subordinate to substantive negotiations, "should be accorded the status and attendant characteristics of a nonmandatory subject of bargaining."); Vanguard Fire & Security Systems, 345 NLRB 1016, 1017-1018 (2005) (employer cannot insist on agenda covering particular points).

3   USF Red Star, 339 NLRB 389, 391 (2003) ("Employees have a protected right under Section 7 of the Act to wear union insignia while working."); Escanaba Paper Co., 314 NLRB 732, 734 (1994) ("no scab," "flex this," and other buttons protected by NLRA).

4   AT&T Connecticut, 356 NLRB No. 118, slip op. at 1-2 (2011).

5   USF Red Star, 339 NLRB 389 (2003).

6   Pathmark Stores, 342 NLRB 378, 379 (2004) (grocery employees T-shirt with slogan "Don't Cheat About the Meat," unprotected).

7   Escanaba Paper Co., 314 NLRB 732, 734 (1994).

8   Sacred Heart Medical Center, 347 NLRB 531, 531-532 (2006).

9   United Parcel Service, 195 NLRB 441, 441 (1972).

10  *See* Holladay Park Hospital, 262 NLRB 278, 279 (1982) (ban on yellow ribbons worn to show support for union bargaining position unlawful where employer previously allowed nurses to wear red ribbons at Christmas; green ribbons on St. Patrick's Day, smile buttons, and buttons saying "Pet me, I purr"); St. Joseph's Hospital, 225 NLRB 348, 348-349 (1976) (hospital that ordered three nurses to remove allegedly controversial union buttons violated Act because it had previously allowed nurse to wear "Kiss me, I'm Irish" button).

11  London Memorial Hospital, 238 NLRB 704, 708 (1978).

12  Saint Vincent's Hospital, 265 NLRB 38, 42 (1982).

13  *See, e.g.,* Tenneco Automotive, Inc., 357 NLRB No. 84, slip op. at 5 (2011) ("It is well settled that a refusal to comply with a directive to cease protected communications does not constitute insubordination."); USF Red Star, 339 NLRB 389, 390-391 (2003) (written warning); Kolkka Tables and Finnish-American Saunas, 335 NLRB 844, 848-850 (2001) (suspension). **Note:** When a ULP charge alleges illegal discipline, the NLRB often "defers" prosecution to the grievance and arbitration process. Although labor arbitrators are not bound by legal precedent, they often uphold NLRA rights. *See* State of Iowa, 112 LA

360 (Jay, Arb. 1999) (hospital may not ban button reading: "When will the shift end?"); Atlanta Newspapers, 57 LA 841 (Crane, Arb. 1971) (employer not justified in discharging employee for refusing repeated orders from foreman to remove union-related badge).

14    Republic Aviation Corp. v. NLRB, 324 U.S. 793 (Sup. Ct. 1945); Poly-America, Inc., 328 NLRB 667, 668 (1999) (employees did not engage in punishable insubordination when they refused to stop distributing union literature and leave employer's outside nonwork area); Tri-County Medical Center, 222 NLRB 1089, 1089 (1976) ("[E]xcept where justified by business reasons, a rule which denies off-duty employees entry to parking lots, gates and other outside nonworking areas will be found invalid."). **Note:** The fact that a lounge or assembly area is partially or occasionally used for work does not provide a basis to prohibit the distribution of union literature. United Parcel Service, 331 NLRB 338, 341 (2000).

15    *See* AMC Air Conditioning Co., 232 NLRB 283, 284 (1977) ("[An employer] cannot lawfully require an employee to secure permission as a precondition to engage, without fear of management interference or retaliation, in protected concerted activities on company property in nonwork areas on the employees' free time."). **Note:** An exception may apply if the union contract says permission must be obtained.

16    DHL Express, 355 NLRB No. 144 slip op. at 8 (2010).

17    Gainesville Mfg. Co., 271 NLRB 1186, 1188 (1984) ("[T]he close presence of the representatives of [the employer] during the handbilling constituted obvious overt and intended surveillance of union activities..."). **Note:** Literature may lose its protected character if it attacks the employer's products or services, disrupts plant discipline, or spreads malicious falsehoods. New York University Medical Center, 261 NLRB 822, 824 (1982).

18    E.R. Carpenter Co., 284 NLRB 273, 275 (1987) (windshields); Mid-Mountain Foods, 332 NLRB 229, 229-230 (2000) (break room); Superior Emerald Park Landfill, LLC, 340 NLRB 449, 457-458 (2003) (lunchroom).

19    Santa Fe Hotel, 331 NLRB 723, 723 (2000).

20    Highland Superstores, 314 NLRB 146, 149 (1994) (handbills asking customers to shop elsewhere not disloyal because they did not "cast

aspersions upon the Company's service or upon the products it delivered to its customers").

21  **Note:** Although the NLRA requires health care unions to provide 10 days notice before picketing or striking, notice is not required for a peaceful rally held away from an institution's entrance. Sheet Metal Workers' Intern. Ass'n, Local 15 v. NLRB, 491 F.3d 429, 439-440 (D.C. Cir. 2007).

22  Miller Industries Towing Equipment, 342 NLRB 1074, 1086-1087 (2004) (employer violated NLRA when it prohibited employees from holding rally and circling through parking lot with signs). **Note:** In Miller Industries, *supra*, the employer argued that the rally was disruptive because working employees gathered at windows to watch. The NLRB rejected the argument because the employer could have easily directed the observers to return to their stations.

23  Hospital Episcopal San Lucas, 319 NLRB 54, 59 (1995) (writing down names); Embarq Corp., 358 NLRB No. 134 slip op. at 3 (2012) (photographs).

24  Wolfie's, 159 NLRB 686, 694-695 (1966) (rejecting employer's contention that to permit employees working on one shift to picket the next is to require the employer "to finance the pickets"); The Mandarin, 223 NLRB 725, 725 (1976) (employer violated Act when it told employees they could not continue working at restaurant if they continued picketing on days off); E.L. Wiegand Div. v. NLRB, 650 F.2d 463, 474 (3d Cir. 1981). **Note:** Picketers may not be treated as strikers and replaced. E.L. Wiegand Div. v. NLRB, 650 F.2d 463, 474 (3d Cir. 1981).

25  Embarq Corp., 358 NLRB No. 134 slip op. at 3 (2012). **Note:** Healthcare unions must give 10 days written notice of the day and time picketing will commence. The union must also notify the Federal Mediation and Conciliation Service (FMCS). **Further note:** Informational picketing outside a hospital administrative building does not require advance notice if the building does not house patient care activity and is not adjacent to such a facility. See Presbyterian Hospital, 285 NLRB 935, 936 (1987).

26  Riverside Cement Co., 296 NLRB 840, 841 (1989).

27  Santa Barbara News-Press, 357 NLRB No. 51, slip op. at page 4 (2011) ("[B]oycott oriented communications, such as the employees'

'Cancel Your Newspaper Today' banner message, do not constitute disloyalty that would result in a loss of the Act's protection."); Highland Superstores, 314 NLRB 146, 146 (1994) (employer violated NLRA by threatening employees with termination for handbilling in support of customer boycott); Circle Bindery, 218 NLRB 861, 861-862 (1975) (discharge illegal where reason was employee's efforts to convince contractor to remove job from employer). **Note:** Employers sometimes threaten to sue unions for "tortious interference with advantageous contractual relations" when they learn of communications with customers. Such a suit would be subject to dismissal in the absence of proof of actual malice. *See* Beverly Hills Foodland, Inc. v. Food & Commercial Workers Local 655, 39 F.3d 191, 196 (8th Cir. 1994) ("Here Foodland has alleged the distribution of the Union handbill tortiously interfered with its business relations with customers. Because the statements within the handbill are afforded protection under federal labor law, the conduct of distributing the handbills must be afforded the same protection."). Some courts have dismissed tortious interference lawsuits on pre-emption grounds. *See* Wilkes-Barre Publishing Co. v. Newspaper Guild of Wilkes-Barre, 647 F.2d 372, 381-382 (3d Cir. 1981), ("[W]here parties to a labor dispute are charged with tortious interference with a collective bargaining agreement, at least in the absence of outrageous or violent conduct, state law causes of action are preempted."); In re Sewell, 690 F.2d 403, 408 (4th Cir. 1982) (NLRA preempts state law claim). **Further note:** Where a lawsuit against a union is not reasonably based, the NLRB may find an unfair labor practice and order the employer to pay for the union's legal expenses. Milum Textile Services Co., 357 NLRB No. 169, slip op. at 3-6 (2011).

28  *See* Tri-County Medical Center, 222 NLRB 1089, 1089 (1976).

29  Poly-America, Inc., 328 NLRB 667, 668 (1999) ("[B]ecause, as found by the judge, the Respondent's no-distribution/no-solicitation rules as applied to its nonwork areas are invalid, the imposition of any discipline for violation of those rules is likewise invalid.").

30  *See* Kolkka Tables and Finnish-American Saunas, 335 NLRB 844, 848-850 (2001) (suspension for repeatedly refusing supervisor's order to remove union stickers from personal toolbox and for refusing to leave facility, unlawful). **Note:** NLRA protections do not apply if the rule appears in the union contract.

31  *See* IUE Local 742 (Randall Bearings), 213 NLRB 824, 825-828 (1974).

32  The Clarion Hotel-Marin, 279 NLRB 481, 492 (1986).

33  *See* Miron & Sons, 358 NLRB No. 78, slip op. at 19-20 (2012).

34  Valley Hospital Medical Center, 351 NLRB 1250, 1254 (2007). **Note:** Monitoring employees internet posts may violate the NLRA's anti-surveillance policies. *See* Flexsteel Industries, 311 NLRB 257, 257 (1993).

35  Lineback v. Printpack, Inc., 979 F. Supp. 831, 840-842 (S.D. Ind. 1997) (letter from local president to customers stating: "I want to alert you to a potentially alarming situation at our plant that could have an impact on the quality of the packaging materials we manufacture for [your Company] … We hope that if the plant's new management provokes a strike, that you will consider withdrawing your patronage, both because we could no longer guarantee the quality of our product and because it would be the right thing to do."); Sacramento Union, 291 NLRB 540, 547-550 (1988) (letter to newspaper's advertisers stating that the union had been trying for a year and a half to get a contract, that the paper's circulation had been declining, and that the newspaper was heading downhill).

36  *See* DHL Express, 355 NLRB No. 144, fn.3 (2010); Prime Time Shuttle International, 314 NLRB 838, 842-43 (1994). *See also* Beverly Hills Foodland, Inc. v. Food & Commercial Workers Local 655, 39 F.3d 191, 196 (8th Cir. 1994) (handbill asking customers to boycott not grounds for tortious interference lawsuit).

37  Professional Porter & Window Cleaning Co., 263 NLRB 136, 139 fn.12 (1982) ("[T]he truth or falsity of a communication is not material and is not the test of its protected character.").

38  Litton Financial Printing Div. v. NLRB, 501 U.S. 190, 198 (U.S. Sup. Ct. 1991). **Note:** A contract provision can grant an employer the right to discontinue a benefit at expiration. To qualify as a waiver, however, the provision must be clear and unmistakable. A provision that simply states that a benefit is effective "for the duration of this agreement" does not permit the employer to make unilateral changes when the contract expires. The Finley Hospital, 359 NLRB No. 9, slip op. at 3 (2012).

39  Bethlehem Steel Co., 136 NLRB 1500, 1502 (1962).

40  WKYC-TV, Inc., 359 NLRB No. 30, slip op. at 8 (2012) (overruling prior decisions, Board stated: "[W]e now hold that an employer, following contract expiration, must continue to honor a dues-checkoff arrangement established in that contract until the parties have either reached agreement or a valid impasse permits unilateral action by the employer."). **Note:** In 2012, an employer challenged the legitimacy of three of President Obama's appointments to the NLRB. This case (Noel Canning v. NLRB) is now at the U.S. Supreme Court and a decision is expected in 2014. If the Court sustains the employer, some of the Board's decisions in 2012-2013, including WKYC-TV, may lose their precedential value — at least until the current or a future Board hears a case with the same issue and issues a ruling to the same effect.

41  KSM Industries, 336 NLRB 133, 143 (2001) ("[P]arties to a collective-bargaining relationship have a continuing statutory obligation to adhere to established grievance procedures even after the expiration of a contract.").

42  Allied Chemical & Alkali Workers of America Local 1 v. Pittsburgh Plate Glass Co., 404 U.S. 157, 185 (U.S. Sup. Ct. 1971).

43  *See* Sacramento Union, 291 NLRB 552, 557 (1988) (deadlock on issue of union security, a major dispute between the parties, did not permit employer to declare impasse and implement final contract offer). **Note:** An exception may apply if impasse on a critical issue creates a complete breakdown in negotiations or if an exigent circumstance having a major economic effect requires the employer to take immediate action.

44  *See* Roosevelt Memorial Medical Center, 348 NLRB 1016, 1016-1017 (2006).

45  **Note:** The Board has ruled that an information request does not have to be answered if it is made for an ulterior motive, for example, to prevent the employer from getting to impasse. ACF Industrial, LLC, 347 NLRB 1040 (2006). Nevertheless, an information request cannot be treated as in bad faith "if at least one reason for the demand can be justified." Island Creek Coal Co., 292 NLRB 480, 489 (1989).

46  *See* Kingsbury, Inc., 355 NLRB No. 195, fn.14 (2010).

47  Goya Foods, Inc., 238 NLRB 1465, 1466-1467 (1978).

48  First National Bank of Omaha, 171 NLRB 1145, 1151 (1968) ("[A] work stoppage does not lose its presumptive protection merely because it is limited in duration.").

49  *See* Frick Co., 161 NLRB 1089, 1108 (1966) (equating strike time to unexcused absence contravenes right of employees to engage in protected strike activity); Quality Castings Co., 139 NLRB 928, 930 (1962) (employer may not treat strike as absence forfeiting employees' right to profit sharing).

50  Savage Gateway Supermarket, 286 NLRB 180, 183 (1987). **Note:** An exception may apply if an employee's surprise absence creates a risk of imminent harm to persons or property.

51  *See* Honolulu Rapid Transit Co., 110 NLRB 1806, 1811 (1954) (suspensions of workers who engaged in four consecutive weekend strikes, lawful).

52  *See* Pacific Telephone Co., 107 NLRB 1547, 1548 (1954). *See also* Farley Candy Co., 300 NLRB 849, 849 (1990) (characterizing intermittent strike as "a plan to strike, return to work, and strike again").

53  Robertson Industries, 216 NLRB 361, 362 (1975) (two strikes over different issues and with different groups of employees participating). *See also* Chelsea Homes, 298 NLRB 813, 831 (1990) ("[T]wo stoppages, even of like nature, are insufficient to constitute evidence of a pattern of recurring, and therefore unprotected stoppages."); NLRB v. Empire Gas, Inc., 566 F.2d 681, 686 (10th Cir. 1977) (one-day walkout followed by two-day stoppage, protected). **Note:** The law is not settled on whether a series of walkouts precipitated by an employer unfair labor practice is protected under Section 7 of the NLRA. Two cases have ruled in the affirmative: Blades Mfg. Corp., 144 NLRB 561, 566, 567 (1963) and Schneider Mills, 164 NLRB 879, 884 fn.17 (1967). One said no. Valley City Furniture Co., 110 NLRB 1589, 1594-1595 (1954).

54  Swope Ridge Geriatric Center, 350 NLRB 64, 67-68 (2007).

55  National Steel and Shipbuilding Co., 324 NLRB 499, 509–510 (1997).

56  *See* U.S. Service Industries, 315 NLRB 285, 285 (1994).

57  New Orleans Roosevelt Corp., 132 NLRB 248, 250 (1961) (employer must establish that it hired permanent replacements before strikers applied for reinstatement); Ramada Inn, 201 NLRB 431, 437 (1973) (return-to-work telegram sent by union four hours after start of one-day strike requires employer to displace subsequently hired replacement). **Note:** An unresolved question concerns the efficacy of a return-to-work offer submitted *before* a short-term strike commences, for

example as part of a health care union's 10-day strike notice. No Board decision has ruled on whether such an offer bars the hiring of permanent replacements, either in advance of or during the strike. However, an NLRB General Counsel advice memorandum takes a negative position. Sidney Square Convalescent Center, 1996 WL 789042, August 30, 1996. It would be prudent to repeat the return-to-work offer when the strike begins.

58 *See* Guard Publ'g Co, 339 NLRB 353, 355 (2003) ("[A] contractual reservation of managerial discretion … does not survive expiration of the contract that contains it, absent evidence that the parties intended it to survive").

59 *See* Bottom Line Enterprises, 302 NLRB 373, 374 (1991) ([W]hen, as here, the parties are engaged in negotiations, an employer's obligation to refrain from unilateral changes extends beyond the mere duty to give notice and an opportunity to bargain; it encompasses a duty to refrain from implementation at all, unless and until an overall impasse has been reached on bargaining for the agreement as a whole."). **Note:** An exception applies when economic exigencies compel prompt action. Even in that case, however, the employer must provide the union with adequate notice and an opportunity to bargain. RBE Electronics of S.D., 320 NLRB 80, 81-82 (1995).

60 Miron & Sons, 358 NLRB No. 78, slip op. at 19 (2012). *See also,* Sunoco, Inc., 349 NLRB 240, 244 (2007) ("An employer's practices, even if not required by a collective-bargaining agreement, which are regular and long-standing, rather than random or intermittent, become terms and conditions of unit employees' employment, which cannot be altered without offering their collective-bargaining representative notice and an opportunity to bargain over the proposed change after change.).

61 The Finley Hospital, 359 NLRB No. 9, slip op. at 5 (2012) (employer violated NLRA "when it informed employees that it would no longer give annual increases following the expiration of the 2005 agreement.").

62 *See, e.g.,* Yale Univ., 330 NLRB 246, 247 (1999) (teaching fellows); Highlands Hosp. Corp., 278 NLRB 1097, 1097 (1986) (security guards); Vencare Ancillary Servs., Inc. v. NLRB, 352 F.3d 318, 324-25 (6th Cir. 2003) (healthcare workers).

63 *But see* City Dodge Center, 289 NLRB 194, 196-197 (1988) (work stoppage protected by Act where employees stopped work and waited peacefully for two to three hours to present complaints to president); Cudahy Packing Co., 29 NLRB 837, 866-868 (1941) (brief stoppage during which employees stood peaceably at or near their work stations, protected).

64 *See* Safety Kleen Oil Services, 308 NLRB 208, 209 (1992) ("The Board has found a sickout to be protected concerted activity in those cases where there is evidence that the employer knew or had reason to know that the employees were not really sick, but were engaged in a work stoppage to protest their working conditions."). **Note:** Employees should not apply for sick pay.

65 *See* Shelly & Anderson Furn. Mfg. Co., 199 NLRB 250, 263-265 (1972).

66 Harvey Mfg., 309 NLRB 465, 468-471 (1992)

67 *See* Sociedad Espanola, 342 NLRB 458, 461-462 (2004) (lockout following 48-hour strike lawful where employer had reasonable grounds to fear that another 48-hour strike was imminent); Bali Blinds Midwest, 292 NLRB 243, 246-247 (1988) (employer can lock out employees who refuse to assure that strikes would not recur during bargaining process).

68 Wayneview Care Center, 356 NLRB No. 30, slip op. at 1 (2010) (lockout unlawful where "there is no evidence that the Union was planning another strike or further picketing"). **Note:** The Board may also find a lockout unlawful if the facts indicate that its purpose was to punish employees for their protected activity. *See* Highland Superstores, 314 NLRB 146, 146 (1994) ("[W]e are persuaded that the Respondent acted to punish the employees for their handbilling, rather than in support of its bargaining position.").

69 **Note:** The address for the FMCS notice is Notice Processing Unit, Federal Mediation and Conciliation Service, 2100 K Street NW, Washington, D.C. 20427. State agency addresses can be found on the Association of Labor Relations Agencies website (www.alra.org). **Further note:** Some states do not offer labor mediation services. In that event, the union need only serve the FMCS. *See* Brotherhood of Locomotive Firemen and Enginemen v. NLRB, 302 F.2d 198, 200-201 (9th Cir. 1962).

70 Local Union 219, Retail Clerks Intern. Assn. v. NLRB, 265 F.2d 814, 819-820 (D.C. Cir. 1959).

71 Mastro Plastics Corp. v. NLRB, 350 U.S. 270, 286-289 (U.S. Sup. Ct. 1956).

72 29 U.S.C. §158(g). **Note:** The 10-day notice rule does not apply to a strike caused by a serious unfair labor practice. Council's Center for Problems of Living, 289 NLRB 1122 fn.3 (1988) ("The judge found, and we agree, that the September 29, 1982 strike [caused by the discharge of several employees] was an unfair labor practice strike. The judge further found, applying the doctrine of Mastro Plastics Corp. v. NLRB, 350 U.S. 270 (1956), that the Respondent Union was excused, because of the nature of the strike, from the notice requirement of Sec. 8(g) of the Act. We agree."). **Further note:** The Board has interpreted the Mastro Plastic exception to apply only when an employer's unfair labor practices are serious and provoke employees into taking spontaneous action. Cedarcrest Inc., 246 NLRB 870, 876 (1979) (unilateral cut in wages).

73 *See* NLRB v. Federal Security, Inc., 154 F.3d 751, 755-757 (7th Cir. 1998) (security guards at a housing complex).

74 Leprino Cheese Mfg. Co., 170 NLRB 601, 606-607 (1968).

75 NLRB v. Borg-Warner Corp., 356 U.S. 342 (1958). **Note:** Generally speaking, mandatory subjects are defined as matters that "vitally affect" wages, hours, and other terms and conditions of employment. Bricklayers (Daniel J. Titulaer), 306 NLRB 229, 235 (1992). All other lawful matters are deemed permissive subjects.

76 Nassau Ins. Co., 280 NLRB 878 fn.3 and 891-892 (1986). **Note:** An exception may apply if the employer voluntarily bargains on the matter. *Cf.* KCET-TV, 312 NLRB 15, 15-16 (1993) (employer could not complain about union's conduct in demanding permissive subject where it failed to demand that subject be removed from table and willingly bargained on it). Another exception may arise if the permissive subject is not a core issue in dispute. *Cf.* ACF Industries, 347 NLRB 1040, 1042 (2006). **Further note:** The fact that a permissive subject is included in the existing or recently expired collective bargaining agreement does not convert the matter to a mandatory subject when bargaining for a successor agreement.

77   *See* Goya Foods, Inc., 238 NLRB 1465, 1466-1467 (1978) (no-strike clause remains in effect for grievances that arose under expired agreement where the agreement includes an applicable arbitration procedure).

78   Thornhill v. State of Alabama, 310 U.S. 88, 102, 105-106 (U.S. Sup. Ct. 1940) ("In the circumstances of our times the dissemination of information concerning the facts of a labor dispute must be regarded as within that area of free discussion that is guaranteed by the Constitution .... The streets are natural and proper places for the dissemination of information and opinion."). **Note:** In some circumstances, a court can classify a privately owned sidewalk as a "public forum," allowing its use for picketing, rallies, and other events. *See* Venetian Casino Resort v. Local Joint Executive Bd. of Las Vegas, 257 F.3d 937, 948 (9th Cir. 2001) (privately owned walkway is public forum where it had historically public character, no alternative public space was available in front of the property, and the walkway was interconnected with publicly-owned sidewalks).

79   *See, e.g.,* Howard Gault Co. v. Texas Rural Legal Aid, Inc., 848 F.2d 544, 561 (5th Cir. 1988) (statute forbidding picketing by more than two persons within 50 feet of an entrance, unconstitutional); United Food & Commercial Workers v. IBP, Inc., 857 F.2d 422, 430-432 (8th Cir. 1988) (statute requiring pickets to stand at least 50 feet from each other, unconstitutional); Edwards v. City of Coeur d'Alene, 262 F.3d 856, 863-867 (9th Cir. 2001) (ordinance banning wooden or plastic supports for picket signs, unconstitutional); Local 391, International Brotherhood of Teamsters v. City of Rocky Mount, 672 F.2d 376, 380 (4th Cir. 1982) (in view of other restrictions in ordinance, permit requirement is unconstitutional).

80   *See* Sprain Brook Manor Nursing Home, 351 NLRB 1190, 1191 (2007) (employer violated Act by calling police to the picket line without a legitimate reason); Gainesville Mfg. Co., 271 NLRB 1186, 1187–1188 (1984).

81   W.S. Butterfield Theatre, 292 NLRB 30, 33-34 (1988) (movie theatre must allow union to picket on private sidewalk where picketing on nearest public property would be ineffective or unsafe); Town & Country Supermarkets, 340 NLRB 1410, 1413-1414 (2004) (store may not forbid picketing on entrances and exitways).

82  *See* Wild Oats Community Markets, 336 NLRB 179, 180-182 (2001). **Note:** An employer violates the NLRA if it asks a third-party owner to evict picketers. Id. at 181-182. **But note:** If the property owner instructs the employer to evict picketers, the employer may have sufficient authority to act as the owner's agent.

83  *See e.g.*, Scott Hudgens, 230 NLRB 414 (1977) (shopping center); Holland Rantos Co., 234 NLRB 726 (1978) (industrial park); Little & Co., 296 NLRB 691 (1989) (office building).

84  Letter Carriers v. Austin, 418 U.S. 264, 283 (U.S. Sup. Ct. 1974) ("[F]ederal law gives a union license to use intemperate, abusive, or insulting language without fear of restraint or penalty if it believes such rhetoric to be an effective means to make its point."); United Parcel Service, 234 NLRB 223, 227-228 (1978) (union newsletter alleging that employer buys arbitrators and judges, protected by NLRA). **Note:** Strikers should be cautious in criticizing the employer's products or services. A knowingly false statement, such as a claim that a product will cause death or severe injury, can be punished as disloyalty. *See* Montefiore Hospital v. NLRB, 621 F.2d 510, 517 (2nd Cir. 1980) (warning that patients would not be taken care of at struck hospital; Coca Cola Bottling Works, 186 NLRB 1050, 1054 (1970) (false claims of mice droppings in soda bottles). **But note:** To lose protection for an act of disloyalty, an employee's criticism must evidence "a malicious motive." *Richboro Community Mental Health Council*, 242 NLRB 1267, 1268 (1979).

85  Steam Press Holdings, Inc. v. Hawaii Teamsters Local 996, 302 F.3d 998, 1006 (9th Cir. 2002).

86  *See* H.W. Barss Co., 296 NLRB 1286, 1286-1288 (1989) (employer violated NLRA by suing union and members for picket signs calling owner a "scab").

87  *See* Ornamental Iron Work Co., 295 NLRB 473, 479 (1989) (in view of "the traditional right of pickets to take steps necessary to perfect a verbal appeal to a driver headed for a strike-bound facility ... an instantaneous blockage, which allows those seeking access to freely choose between disregarding or honoring the picket line, fails to convert protected into unprotected strike action.").

88  *See, e.g.*, Airo Die Casting, 347 NLRB 810 (2004) (employer violated NLRA by discharging striker for obscene gesture accompanied by obscene utterance and racial epithet).

89 Detroit Newspaper Agency, 342 NLRB 223, 293 (2004). *See also* Santa Barbara News-Press, 357 NLRB No. 51, slip op. at 11 (2011) ("The mere fact that an otherwise peaceful concerted action might be illegal under local law does not necessarily remove it from the Act's protection.").

90 **Note:** Picketers can ask shared-site employees not to provide services or give other direct assistance to the struck employer. *See* Electrical Workers Local 3 (New Power Wire), 144 NLRB 1089, 1094-1095 (1963).

91 *See* Electrical Workers Local 3 (New Power Wire), 144 NLRB 1089, 1094 (1963).

92 29 U.S.C. §160(*l*).

93 29 U.S.C. §187.

94 Local 761, International Union of Electrical Workers v. NLRB, 366 U.S. 667, 673 (U.S. Sup. Ct. 1961).

95 Anchortank, Inc. v. NLRB, 601 F.2d 233, 240 (5th Cir. 1979) ("A striking union may supplement its picketing of the premises with non-situs requests to honor the picket line directed to the same employees who ordinarily would encounter the pickets."). *See also* Teamsters Local 200 (Milwaukee Plywood), 126 NLRB 650, 650 (1960) (outside union does not violate NLRA by instructing members to observe picket line at customer facility).

96 **Note:** One of the largest strikebreaking firms, AFIMAC, advertises on the internet that "Our strike security and labor dispute management team can assist a client's legal team by gathering evidence to obtain injunctions and temporary restraining orders."

97 29 U.S.C. §§106-108 (*Norris-LaGuardia Anti-Injunction Act*).

98 *See* 29 U.S.C §§178-180.

99 **Note:** Employee communications with financial analysts are protected by the NLRA even if they cause a crisis for the employer. A communication may lose protection, however, if it conveys knowingly false information. *See* Dresser-Rand Co., 358 NLRB No. 34 fn.2 (2012) ("Initially, we agree with the judge, for the reasons stated in his decision, that Painter's calls to the stock analysts constituted protected, concerted activity. But we also agree with the judge that Painter lost the Act's protection by [incorrectly] stating during the calls that the workload at the Respondent's Olean facility had dropped by 50 percent.").

100 *See* 29 U.S.C. §158(d) (4) (employee's loss of status for failure to provide notice "shall terminate if and when he is reemployed by such employer").

101 *See* NLRB v. Florida Dept. of Bus. Reg., 868 F.2d 391, 394-396 (11th Cir. 1989).

102 Youngstown Sheet and Tube Co., 238 NLRB 1082, 1084-1085 (1978).

103 *See* Mosher Steel Co., 220 NLRB 336, 336 (1975).

104 Preterm, Inc., 240 NLRB 654, 656 (1979).

105 Lundy Packing Co., 223 NLRB 139, 156-157 (1976) ("[T]here was nothing improper in an arrangement whereby additional employees would be called upon to join the strike as the strike progressed.").

106 *See* Local 761, Intern. Union of Elec., Radio and Mach. Workers v. NLRB, 366 U.S. 667 (1961).

107 *See* Central Soya Co., 288 NLRB 1402, 1406 (1988).

108 Building & Construction Trades Council (Markwell & Hartz), 155 NLRB 319 (1965) (more union-favorable *Moore Dry Dock* standards apply).

109 *See* Ornamental Iron Work Co., 295 NLRB 473, 479 (1989).

110 *See* Electrical Workers Local 1150 (Cory Corp.), 84 NLRB 972, 976 (1949) (2000 picketers). **Note:** An employer can sue a union for business losses resulting from illegal mass picketing. *See* Rainbow Tours, Inc. v. Hawaii Joint Council of Teamsters, 704 F.2d 1443 (9th Cir. 1983).

111 Genesco, Inc. v. Joint Council 13, United Shoe Workers, 230 F.Supp. 923, 931 (S.D.N.Y. 1964) ("Mass picketing stands on the same footing with other picketing as long as it does not block access to and from the struck premises or does not threaten physical violence.").

112 *See* Deister Concentrator Co., 253 NLRB 358, 393 (1980) ("When employees engage in a strike they must accept certain risks, and one of those risks is that their exercise of economic power may not be successful, but rather may, under certain circumstances, be counterproductive. The Act guarantees employees a right to engage in concerted activity. It does not guarantee that such activity will be successful, nor does not it prohibit an employer from making economic adjustments in consequence of the results caused by the strike.").

113 Service Employees (Our Lady of Perpetual Hope Nursing Home), 208 NLRB 117, 119 (1974).

114 National Steel & Shipbuilding Co., 324 NLRB 499, 535 (1977) ("[I]t may be presumed that the mere presence of the camera will inhibit or chill [employees] in saying or doing things that are nevertheless protected by Section 7."). **Note:** Surveillance of concerted activity is unlawful irrespective of whether employees know of it, and even though not authorized by top management. Starbrite Furniture Corp., 226 NLRB 507, 510 (1976). **Further note:** The continued regular operation of a previously installed security system during a strike does not violate the NLRA even if it records concerted activity.

115 Horsehead Resource Development Co. v. NLRB, 154 F.3d 328, 341 (6th Cir. 1998) ("The surveillance of union members who were in no way engaged with company personnel or property, but were merely talking among themselves or moving to and from the picket shack and the portable restroom, was unjustified."); Russell Sportswear Corp., 197 NLRB 1116, 1117-1118 (1972).

116 Williamhouse-Regency of Delaware, 297 NLRB 199, 199 (1989) ("It is well settled that an offer, once made, remains on the table unless explicitly withdrawn by the offeror or unless circumstances arise that would reasonably lead the parties to believe that the offer had been withdrawn.").

117 Romal Iron Works Corp., 285 NLRB 1178, 1182 (1989) (racial slurs); Domsey Trading Corp., 310 NLRB 777, 793 (1993) (calling strikers "whores" and "monkeys").

118 *See* Facet Enterprises, 290 NLRB 152, 153 (1988).

119 Gloversville Embossing Corp., 297 NLRB 182, 187-190 (1989). *See also* S & W Motor Lines, 236 NLRB 938, 951–952 (1978) (offering a premium for the alleged risks involved in crossing a picket line).

120 29 U.S.C. §504(a).

121 Fairfield Tower Condominium Assn., 343 NLRB 923, 924 (2004).

122 Land Air Delivery, 286 NLRB 1131, 1132 (1987) ("T]he Respondent's permanent contracting out of the work previously performed by bargaining unit employees without notifying and bargaining with the Union constituted an unfair labor practice, even though done in the course of a strike."). *See* Naperville Ready Mix v. NLRB, 242 F.3d 744, 756 (7th Cir. 2001) ("[T]he mere fact that employees go on strike does not relieve the employer of the duty to bargain to impasse, and thus it does not permit an employer permanently to subcontract out unit work in the absence of an impasse.").

123 *See* American Cyanamid Co., 235 NLRB 1316, 1323 (1978).

124 Land Air Delivery, 286 NLRB 1131, 1132 fn.8 (1987) ("An employer is not under a duty to bargain over temporary subcontracting necessitated by a strike where such subcontracting does not transcend reasonable measures necessary to maintain operations in strike circumstances.").

125 *See* Fibreboard Paper Products Corp. v. NLRB, 379 U.S. 203 (U.S. Sup. Ct. 1964).

126 20 C.F.R. §652.9(a).

127 29 U.S.C. §158(b) (4) (B). *See* ILA Local 799 (Allied International), 257 NLRB 1075, 1078-1079 (1981) (strike to protest invasion of Afghanistan, unlawful secondary boycott).

128 See Ritchie v. United Mine Workers of America, 410 F.2d 827 (6th Cir. 1969) (overturning jury finding that union was responsible for destruction of coal tipple). **But note:** A union may be found liable for failing to take steps to stop or prevent known misconduct. Local 248, Meat & Allied Food Workers (Milwaukee Independent Meat Packers Assn.), 222 NLRB 1023, 1023 (1976) (union accountable for acts of violence on picket line where officers knew of misconduct but made no serious attempt to curtail it).

129 NLRB v. Fruit and Vegetable Packers, Local 760, 377 U.S. 58 (U.S. Sup. Ct. 1964).

130 AFTRA Local 55 (Great Western Broadcasting), 150 NLRB 467, 472 (1964).

131 *See, e.g.*, Great American, 322 NLRB 17, 23-24 (1996); Sandusky Mall, Co., 329 NLRB 618, 620-622 (1999); Wal-Mart Stores, 340 NLRB 1216, 1216-1217 (2003).

132 *See* Teamsters Local 560 (Curtin Matheson Scientific) 248 NLRB 1212, 1213 (1980) (citing Senator Taft's statement that "The secondary boycott ban is merely intended to prevent a union from injuring a third person who is not involved in any way in the dispute or strike ... It is not intended to apply to a case where the third party is, in effect, in cahoots with or acting as a part of the primary employer.").

133 Southern Council of Industrial Workers (Missoula White Pine Sash Co.), 301 NLRB 410 fn.3 (1991).

134 Los Angeles Newspaper Guild Local 69 (Hearst Corp.), 185 NLRB 303, 304-305 (1970).

135 National Maritime Union Local 333 (D. M. Picton & Co.), 131 NLRB 693, 699 (1961). **Note:** The D.C. Circuit Federal Court of Appeals takes a broader approach, finding ally status when a customer makes the arrangements. Laborers Local 859 v. NLRB, 446 F.2d 1319, 1321 (D.C. Cir. 1971). **Further note:** When a customer arranges for another entity to take over the work, the new entity may be deemed an ally if the struck employer is substantially involved. Mount Morris Graphic Arts, 219 NLRB 1030, 1032 (1975).

136 Central Illinois Public Service Co., 326 NLRB 928, 995 (1998).

137 International Longshoremen's Ass'n (Coastal Stevedoring), 313 NLRB 412, 415-417 (1993).

138 International Longshoremen's Ass'n. v. NLRB, 56 F.3d 205, 213 (D.C. Cir. 1995).

139 *See* Teamsters Local 324 (Truck Operators League of Oregon), 122 NLRB 25, 27 (1958).

140 *See* Oil, Chemical and Atomic Workers (Petroleum Maintenance Co.), 223 NLRB 757, 758-759 (1976) (temporary employment agency functioned as a "direct and integrated part" of struck employer's operations).

141 IBEW Local 399 (Illinois Bell), 235 NLRB 555, 555 (1978). *See also* Teamsters Local 70 (Dept. of Defense), 288 NLRB 1224, 1225 (1988) (threat to picket Department of Defense not unlawful where DOD triggered labor dispute by transferring forklift work from contractor to in-house).

142 *See* Carpenters Local 1098 (Womack, Inc.), 280 NLRB 875 (1986).

143 *See* Frisby v. Schultz, 487 U.S. 474, 483 (U.S. Sup. Ct. 1988) (interpreting town ordinance forbidding picketing "before or about the residence or dwelling of any individual" to permit walking in front of an entire block of houses).

144 *See* Kirkeby v. Furness, 92 F.3d 655, 661 (8th Cir. 1996).

145 Sailors Union of the Pacific (Moore Dry Dock Co.), 92 NLRB 547, 549 (1950).

146 Teamsters Local 200 (Reilly Cartage), 183 NLRB 305, 305 (1970).

147 Teamsters Local 83 (Allied Concrete), 231 NLRB 1097, 1098 (1977).

148 IBEW Local 861 (Plauche Electric), 135 NLRB 250, 255 (1962).

149 Teamsters Local 379 (Catalano Bros.), 175 NLRB 459, 461 (1969)

(asking secondary employees not to unload truck "amounted to no more than lawful requests to honor a primary picket line").

150 P.B.&S. Chemical Co., 321 NLRB 525, 525 (1996) (employees who honor picket lines are protected from discharge whether their motive is to show support, to remain neutral, or to avoid an unpleasant confrontation). **Note:** Sympathy strikers can lose their NLRA protections if they honor picket lines intermittently rather than continuously. *See* Pacific Telephone & Telegraph Co., 107 NLRB 1547, 1550-1551 (1954). **Further note:** NLRA protections do not apply to supervisors and managers.

151 Mastro Plastics Corp. v. NLRB, 350 U.S. 270, 283 (U.S. Sup. Ct. 1956); Pilot Freight Carriers, 224 NLRB 341, 342 fn.6 (1976).

152 Arlan's Dep't Store of Michigan, 133 NLRB 802, 808 (1961).

153 Codified as 29 U.S.C. §143.

154 *See* Plain Dealer Pub. Co. v. Cleveland Typographical Union, 520 F.2d 1220, 1229 (6th Cir. 1975). *See also,* West Penn Power Co., 89 LA 1227, 1231 (Hogler, Arb. 1987) (employees who refused to cross picket line due to safety considerations did not violate no-strike clause); Joseph T. Ryerson & Son, 41 LA 52 (Lynch, Arb. 1963) (refusal to cross picket line, where threats of violence had occurred, in absence of uniformed policemen or any guarantee of personal safety by employer, did not violate no-strike provision).

155 *See* Kingsbury, Inc., 355 NLRB No. 195, fn.14 (2010).

156 Operating Engineers Local 39 (Kaiser Foundation), 268 NLRB 115 fn.1 (1983).

157 Service Employees Local 200 (Eden Park Nursing Home), 263 NLRB 400, 401-402 (1982).

158 *See* In re Teamsters Local 890, 225 B.R. 719 (N.D. Cal. 1998).

159 Edward J. DiBartolo Corp. v. Florida Gulf Coast Bldg. & Const. Trades Council, 485 U.S. 568, 583-588 (U.S. Sup. Ct. 1988) (construction union did not violate NLRA when it distributed handbills urging the public not to patronize neutral businesses within shopping mall). **Note:** Despite widespread misinformation, the term "secondary boycott," does not appear in the NLRA.

160 *See* Carpenters Local 1506 (Eliason & Knuth), 355 NLRB No. 159, slip op. at 5 (2010) (union publicity activity lawful "even when the

object of the activity is to induce the secondary to cease doing business with a primary employer").

161 *See* Carpenters Local 1976 v. NLRB, 357 U.S. 93, 99 (U.S. Sup. Ct. 1958) ("[A] union is free to approach an employer to persuade him to engage in a boycott, so long as it refrains from the specifically prohibited means of coercion through inducement of employees.").

162 *See* Sandusky Mall Co., 329 NLRB 618, 623 (1999) (mall owner that permitted charitable, civic, and other organizations to solicit on its concourse unlawfully barred union handbillers).

163 Service Employees Local 399 (Delta Air Lines), 293 NLRB 602, 602-603 (1989).

164 Carpenters Local 1506 (Eliason and Knuth), 355 NLRB No. 159 (2010) (banners 3-4 feet high and 15-20 feet long).

165 Carpenters Local 1506 (Eliason and Knuth), 355 NLRB No. 159, slip op. at 15 (2010) ("The expansive definition of 'labor dispute' contained in Section 2(9) of the Act easily encompasses both primary and secondary disputes.").

166 Sheet Metal Workers Local 15 (Brandon Regional Medical Center), 356 NLRB No. 162, slip op. at 2-5 (2011).

167 *See* Chicago Typographical Union No. 16 (Alden Press, 151 NLRB 1666, 1669 (1965). **Note:** Brief rallies or demonstrations can be held in front of a secondary employer if there are no signs and no entrances are blocked. *See* Service Employees Local 525 (General Maintenance Co.), 329 NLRB 638, 677, 683 (1999) (no Section 8(b)(4) violation where 20 to 25 participants held evening rallies at secondary or when 40 to 50 demonstrators wearing justice for janitors uniforms marched to building); Sheet Metal Workers Local 15 v. NLRB, 491 F.3d 429, 436-439 (D.C. Cir. 2007) (mock funeral nearly 100 feet from secondary's entrance not coercive).

168 *See* Beverly Hills Foodland, Inc. v. Food & Commercial Workers Local 655, 39 F.3d 191, 196 (8th Cir. 1994).

169 Service Employees Local 525 (General Maintenance Co.), 329 NLRB 638, 639 (1999).

170 Sheet Metal Workers Local 15 (University of South Florida), NLRB Advice Memorandum, October 26, 2009.

171 29 U.S.C. §158(b) (4) (proscribing secondary picketing by a labor organization "or its agents").

172 Trading Port, 219 NLRB 298, 299 fn.3 (1975) ("[T]he nonpayment of benefits to strikers during their period of striking is not a matter about which a company has an obligation to bargain.").

173 Reed National Corp. v. Director of DES, 473 N.E.2d 190, 192 (Mass. 1985).

174 Hertz Corp. v. Acting Director of DET, 771 N.E.2d 153, 157 (Mass. 2002).

175 *See* Bridgestone/Firestone, Inc. v. Employment Appeal Board, 570 N.W.2d 85, 95 (Iowa 1997).

176 *See* Tex-Tan Welhausen Co., 172 NLRB 851, 890 (1968) ("It is found that Respondent's denial of vacation pay to the strikers on the basis of their absence while striking was discriminatory and coerced the employees in the exercise of their rights under the Act.").

177 Conoco, Inc., 265 NLRB 819, 821-822 (1982). **Note:** A contrary result may arise if picketing violates the employee's claimed medical restrictions.

178 Hot Shoppes, 146 NLRB 802, 805 (1964); Avery Heights, 350 NLRB 214, 217 (2007). *See also*, New England Health Care Employees Union v. NLRB, 448 F.3d 189, 195-196 (2nd Cir. 2006) (deliberate attempt to keep permanent replacements secret infers illicit intent to break union).

179 Bernard Dalsin Mfg. Co., 2009 WL 1886693, NLRB Div. of Judges, June 30, 2009 (no appeal taken).

180 **Note:** An employer may not pay replacements more than it offered the union at the bargaining table unless it can prove that it was unable to recruit at the offered rate. Burlington Homes, 246 NLRB 1029, 1030 (1979) ("[The employer's] conduct in offering a higher starting wage to striker replacements had a potentially devastating impact upon the right of employees to strike."). *See also* Beverly Health & Rehabilitation Services, 335 NLRB 635, 638 (2001) (employer violated NLRA by advertising wage rates for strike replacements above those offered to bargaining unit).

181 *See* Grinnell Fire Protection Systems Co. 332 NLRB 1257, 1257-1258 (2000) (union entitled to information regarding strike replacements

due to possibility that they may become part of bargaining unit). **Note:** An employer's obligation to supply names and addresses of temporary replacements is not clear. *Compare* Titan Tire Co., 333 NLRB 1156, 1166-1167 (2001) *with* Safeway Stores, 268 NLRB 284, 285 (1983). **Pointer:** When requesting information about temporaries, specify a reason for needing the data, for example, to learn whether the employer is paying higher wages than it offered the union during contract negotiations.

182 Advertisers Composition Co., 253 NLRB 1019, 1023 (1981).

183 *See* Chicago Tribune Co., 303 NLRB 682, 687 (1991).

184 Fry Foods, 241 NLRB 76, 92 (1979). **Note:** An employer that reaches a good-faith impasse with the union on a new contract can apply its final offer to non-strikers and crossovers.

185 *See* Champ Corp., 291 NLRB 803, 876-877 (1988); Ryan Iron Works, 332 NLRB 506, 507-508 (2000).

186 Pattern Makers' League of North America v. NLRB, 473 U.S. 95, 104-105 (U.S. Sup. Ct. 1985). **Note:** A requirement that a resignation be in writing is valid. Pattern & Model Makers Assn. of Warren (Michigan Model Manufacturers), 310 NLRB 929, 930 (1993). But a requirement that the resignation be sent by U.S. mail is not. UAW Local 449 (Nat. Metalcrafters), 283 NLRB 182, 185 (1987).

187 Armored Transp., Inc., 339 NLRB 374, 377 (2003) ("The law is clear that an employer may not solicit its employees to circulate or sign decertification petitions").

188 Columbia Portland Cement Co. v. NLRB, 979 F.2d 460, 464 (6th Cir. 1992) ("[A]n employer cannot lawfully withdraw recognition from a union if it has committed as yet unremedied unfair labor practices that reasonably tended to contribute to employee disaffection from the union.").

189 *See* Wahl Clipper Corp., 195 NLRB 634, 636 (1972).

190 **Note:** Under some circumstances an employer can petition for a decertification election.

191 *See* NLRB v. Neuro Affiliates Co., 702 F.2d 184, 186-188 (9th Cir. 1983).

192  18 U.S.C. §1231.

193  **Note:** Because an amnesty clause is a "permissive" subject of bargaining, the union cannot insist on the clause as a condition of ending the strike.

194  *See Just Cause, A Union Guide to Winning Discipline Cases* by Robert M. Schwartz (Work Rights Press, 2012).

195  *See, e.g.,* Western Die Casting Co., 79 LA 391, 394 (Koven, 1982) (throwing orange juice at employee, blocking truck for 25 minutes, and approaching strikebreaker with closed fist does not warrant discharge because "it cannot be called destructive or seriously threatening."); Carlisle Corp., 87 LA 103, 105 (Feldman, 1986) (discharge for throwing rocks improper since they did not strike anyone); General Telephone Co. of Kentucky, 69 LA 351 (Bowles, 1977) (assaulting security guard, threatening contractor, and kicking company truck not grounds to deny reinstatement).

196  United States Pipe and Foundry Co., 52 LA 1112, 1115-1116 (Finley, 1969).

197  *See* Georgia-Pacific Corp., 87 LA 188, 192 (Gibson, 1986) (carrying toy gun on picket line "was not as bad as some of the other strike activity for which little or no disciplinary action was taken"); General Telephone Co. of Kentucky, 69 LA 351, 354-355 (Bowles, 1977) (discharge too severe for assault on security guard since employee was part of group and singling him out for disciplinary action would be unfair).

198  Chesapeake Plywood, 294 NLRB 201, 203 fn.9 (1989) (Responding to union contention that the discharge of certain strikers was unlawful because the employer failed to discharge a striker ("Roberts") who engaged in similar misconduct, Board explained: "Because Roberts and the strikers who were discharged by the Respondent were all similarly engaged in strike activity, any variance in discipline within this group of employees would be insufficient as evidence to show that the disciplined employees were treated disparately because of their protected activity."). **But note:** NLRB judges sometimes cite disparate treatment among strikers as evidence that the employer did not have an honest belief that the employee's conduct warranted discharge. *See* Black Angus of Lauderhill, 213 NLRB 425, 433 (1974).

199  *See* Charter International Oil Co., 75 LA 929. 935-936 (Milentz, 1980) (throwing steel ball bearings through window of guard shack not

grounds for discharge in view of employee's prior record, nonviolent nature, and satisfactory work performance).

200 *See* A. Finkl & Sons, 90 LA 502, 509 (Wolff, 1988) (employer's destruction of strikers' shanty).

201 *See* DACCO, 114 LA 1517, 1522 (Shieber, 2000) ("The Arbitrator finds that the Company's failure to give Grievant an opportunity to respond to the charge against him that he had thrown urine at non-strikers before he was discharged, violated Grievant's contractual right to due process, which is a component of the Company's undertaking to only discipline employees for 'just cause.'").

202 Vulcan-Hart Corp., 262 NLRB 167, 168 (1982) (unlawful discharges lead "inexorably to the prolongation of a dispute").

203 Consumers Power Co., 282 NLRB 130, 132 (1986) ("[W]hen an employee is discharged for conduct that is part of the res gestae of protected concerted activities, the relevant question is whether the conduct is so egregious as to take it outside the protection of the Act, or of such a character as to render the employee unfit for further service.").

204 Clear Pine Mouldings, 268 NLRB 1044, 1045-1047 (1984) (threats included telling a nonstriking employee that she was taking her life in her hands, that an employee's house might be burned, and that the hands of certain employees should be broken).

205 Leasco, Inc., 289 NLRB 549 fn.1 (1988) (statement that "If you're taking my truck, I'm kicking your ass right now," constitutes colloquialism that standing alone does not threaten actual physical harm); Service Employees Local 87 (Pacific Telephone), 279 NLRB 168, 178 (1986).

206 Catalytic, Inc., 275 NLRB 97, 98 (1985). *See, e.g.,* Calliope Designs, 297 NLRB 510, 521-522 (1989) ("whore," "prostitute"); Airo Die Casting, 347 NLRB 810, 812 (2006) ("Lawson's conduct on the picket line, the use of obscene language and gestures and a racial slur, standing alone without any threats or violence, did not rise to the level where he forfeited the protection of the Act.").

207 Dreis & Krump Mfg. Co., 221 NLRB 309, 315 (1975).

208 *See* Montgomery Ward & Co. v. NLRB, 374 F.2d 606, 608 (10th Cir. 1967) (member of the public entitled to far higher degree of control from picket than strikebreaker or non-striking employee).

209 *See* Dowd v. United Steelworkers of America, Local No. 286, 253 F.3d 1093 (8th Cir. 2001).

210 Tube Craft, 287 NLRB 491, 492-493 (1987) (blocking incidents lasting 65, 50, and 15 minutes).

211 *See e.g.,* Detroit Newspapers, 342 NLRB 223, 291-294 (2004) (trespass); Newport News Shipbuilding, 265 NLRB 716, 720 (1982) (breach of peace and possession of marijuana); Dresser-Rand Co., 358 NLRB No. 97 (2012). *Cf.* NLRB v. Cambria Clay Prod. Co., 215 F.2d 48, 54 (6th Cir. 1954) ("It is not the fact that there was a violation of the injunction that determines whether [the strikers] should or should not be reinstated, but the type of conduct they engaged in, and the manner and nature and seriousness of their violation of the order.").

212 NLRB v. Thayer Co., 213 F.2d 748 (1st Cir. 1954).

213 Aztec Bus Lines, 289 NLRB 1021, 1027-1029 (1988). *See also* Domsey Trading Corp., 310 NLRB 777, 778 (1993) (discharge of two employees for pushing and shoving non-strikers unlawful because non-striker who assaulted two other strikers not punished). **Note:** Double standards between *strikers* is not a defense in an NLRB proceeding. Chesapeake Plywood, 294 NLRB 201, 203 fn.9 (1989). An exception applies if strike leaders are treated more harshly than rank-and-filers. Lectromelt Casting Co., 278 NLRB 696, 697 fn.13 (1986) ("[T]he underlying principle is that, absent waiver, union office cannot serve as a differentiation basis in discipline."). Moreover, double standards between strikers may lead to a finding that the employer did not have a reasonable belief that the striker committed serious misconduct. *See* Black Angus of Lauderhill, 213 NLRB 425, 433 (1974).

214 KSM Industries, 336 NLRB 133, 143 (2001) ("[P]arties to a collective-bargaining relationship have a continuing statutory obligation to adhere to established grievance procedures even after the expiration of a contract."); NTN Bower Corp., 356 NLRB No. 141, slip op. at 111 (2011) ("[I]nformation concerning alleged strike misconduct is necessary and relevant to the Union's proper performance of its duties.").

215 KSM Industries, 336 NLRB 133, 145 (2001).

216 *See* KSM Industries, 336 NLRB 133, 142-143 (2001) ("With respect to the request for information, I find that the Union's April 4 explanation to the Respondent that it needed the records of discipline given to replacement workers during the strike to determine whether KSM has

applied discipline in a disparate fashion, to be a legitimate and proper request.").

217 *See* Iowa Beef Processors, 255 NLRB 1328 fn.3 (1981) ("Like the Administrative Law Judge, we are satisfied that Respondent's effort to explain and justify its refusal to reinstate striker Lewis by relying on this incident is undermined by the following factors: the long and unexplained delay between the incident that assertedly caused the discharge and the date of the discharge itself."); University of New Mexico, 125 LA 1013, 1017 (Blackard, Arb. 2008) ("A second principle of industrial due process is that employers must impose discipline within a reasonable time after learning of misconduct unless there is an acceptable reason for a delay."). *But see* Tube Craft, 287 NLRB 491, 491 (1987) (one-year delay not fatal where, at time misconduct transpired, employer told union it was reserving right to take disciplinary action).

218 Hormigonera Del Toa, 311 NLRB 956, 957–958 and fn.3 (1993). *See also* The Grosvenor Resort, 350 NLRB 1197, 1198 (2007) (absent circumstances justifying a longer delay, striker must begin search for work within two weeks of discharge).

219 *See* Aztec Bus Lines, 289 NLRB 1021, 1029 (1988) ("[W]e cannot conclude that the Respondent can lawfully deny [strikers] reinstatement in the face of its failure … to make thorough inquiries into apparent misconduct by other non-strikers.").

220 *See* Freemont Medical Center, 357 NLRB No. 158, slip op. at 7-8 (2011).

221 *See, e.g.*, Spurlino Materials, LLC, 357 NLRB No. 126, slip op. at 11-15 (2011) (termination of union supporter); RGC (USA) Mineral Sands, 332 NLRB 1633 1633-1634 (2001) (discriminatory job assignments); Genstar Stone Products, 317 NLRB 1293, 1294 (1995) (failure to provide requested information); Child Development Council of Northeastern Pennsylvania, 316 NLRB 1145, 1146 (1995) (illegal threat to hire permanent replacements).

222 Vulcan-Hart Corp., 262 NLRB 167, 168 (1982) (discharge of strikers).

223 **Note:** Lack of work does not qualify as a legitimate and substantial justification unless the employer makes diligent efforts to regain its lost business. Pace Motor Lines, 260 NLRB 1395, 1411 (1982) (failure to reinstate unlawful where employer "voluntarily curtailed its business operations and did not in good faith attempt to recoup its prestrike cus-

tomers in order to further discourage or block employee union activities"). **Further note:** A permanent subcontract of bargaining unit work may not be a justification if the employer failed to give the union prior notice of the decision or an opportunity to bargain. American Cyanamid, Co., 235 NLRB 1316, 1321-1323 (1978).

224 Kraft Foods North America, 355 NLRB No. 156, slip op. at 2-3 (2010); Peterbilt Motors Co., 357 NLRB No. 13, slip op. at 2-3 (2011).

225 Stamco Division, Monarch Machine Tool Co., 227 NLRB 1265, 1268 (1977) (ordering company to "supply the Union, its auditors, and accountants, with all books and records containing financial information relevant to the substantiation of [the employer's] claim that it is financially unable to meet the Union's economic demands").

226 National Extrusion & Mfg. Co., 357 NLRB No. 8, slip op. at 1-4 (2011).

227 See AFL Quality NY LLC, 2013 WL 819360, NLRB Division of Judges, March 5, 2013.

228 Houchens Mkt. of Elizabethtown, 155 NLRB 729, 734 (1965).

229 ServiceNet, Inc., 340 NLRB 1245, 1246-47 (2003).

230 See Daycon Prod. Co., 357 NLRB No. 92, slip op. at 11-12 (2011). **Note:** A bona fide impasse occurs when both parties understand that they have reached a deadlock in negotiations, there are no realistic prospects that further discussions will prove fruitful, and the employer has answered all union information requests on issues separating the parties.

231 See, e.g., Child Development Council of Northeastern Pennsylvania, 316 NLRB 1145, 1145 (1995) (threats); Spurlino Materials, LLC, 357 NLRB No. 126, slip op. at 9-14 (2011) (unlawful discharge).

232 NLRB Casehandling Manual §10266.2 ("In cases involving an unfair labor practice accompanied by a strike allegedly in protest thereof, the Regional Office should determine the nature of the strike. If the evidence supports a finding of an unfair labor practice strike, the Regional Office should allege such status in the complaint and seek an open-ended order requiring the reinstatement, on application, of all qualified striking employees."). **Note:** Although the NLRB is more likely to classify a stoppage as a ULP strike if it occurs on the heels of an unfair labor practice, this is not an absolute requirement. ULP status can be

awarded to strikes that protest violations that occurred weeks or even months in the past. R&H Coal Co., 309 NLRB 28, 28-29 (1992) (13 months). *See* Burns Motor Freight, 250 NLRB 276, 277-278 (1980) ("[T]iming is significant but not conclusive in establishing the basis for a strike.").

233 *See* Outdoor Venture Corp., 327 NLRB 706, 709 (1999).

234 Spurlino Materials, LLC, 357 NLRB No. 126, slip op. at 12 (2011). *See also* F. L. Thorpe, 315 NLRB 147, 150 fn.8 (1994) ("The strike was no less an unfair labor practice strike because the employees discussed whether they would receive the added protection accorded unfair labor practice strikers rather than whether a strike would cure those unfair labor practices.").

235 *See* New Orleans Roosevelt Corp., 132 NLRB 248, 250 (1961); Clow Water Systems Co., 317 NLRB 126, 128 (1995).

236 *See* Dresser-Rand Co., 358 NLRB No. 97, slip op. at 30 (2012) (union communication to members that "While the strike is ended, the struggle continues," does not permit employer to reject union return-to-work offer).

237 *See* Tenneco Automotive, 357 NLRB No. 84, slip op. at 47-48 (2011).

238 **Note:** In a ULP strike, the employer is allowed a five-day grace period to dismiss permanent replacements who are holding strikers' positions.

239 *See* Hotel Holiday Inn De Isla Verde, 259 NLRB 496, 503 (1981).

240 *See* Marchese Metal Industries, 313 NLRB 1022, 1034 (1994).

241 Jones Plastic & Engineering Co., 351 NLRB 61, 64-67 (2007).

242 *See* Jones Plastic & Engineering Co., 351 NLRB 61, 64-66 (2007).

243 **Note:** ULP strikers who refuse to return until all strikers are invited back do not lose their reinstatement rights. Southwestern Pipe, 179 NLRB 364, 365 (1969) ("A striker may refuse an offer of reinstatement, without losing his status as a striker, because the employer has not made a similar offer to other strikers who are also entitled to immediate reinstatement.").

244 **Note:** In addition to wages, a non-reinstated ULP striker is entitled to compensation for vacations, overtime, contributions to pension funds, and out-of-pocket medical expenses. Master Iron Craft Corp., 289 NLRB 1087, 1088 (1988).

245 *See, e.g.,* John Morrell & Co. v. South Dakota Dept. of Labor Unemployment Ins. Div., 460 N.W.2d 141, 143-145 (S.D. Sup. Ct. 1990); In re Sarvis, 251 S.E.2d 434, 437-438 (N.C. Sup. Ct. 1979).

246 **Note:** It is unlawful to insist that a returning striker promise not to rejoin the strike. *See* Dayton Newspapers, 339 NLRB 650, 653 (2003).

247 Am. Ship Bldg. Co. v. NLRB, 380 U.S. 300, 310-313 (U.S. Sup. Ct. 1965).

248 *Id.* at 318.

249 *See* Branch Intern. Services, 310 NLRB 1092, 1104) (1993) ("While it is a legitimate bargaining position to demand or request that the Union acquiesce in a change of the unit, it is not lawful to lock out union employees in furtherance of that demand rather than seeking Board action.").

250 Anderson Enterprises, 329 NLRB 760, 765 (1999).

251 Dayton Newspapers, 339 NLRB 650, 656 (2003) ("[A] fundamental principle underlying a lawful lockout is that the Union must be informed of the employer's demands, so that the Union can evaluate whether to accept them and obtain reinstatement.").

252 *See* Dayton Newspapers, 339 NLRB 650, 657-658 (2003); Alden Leeds, 357 NLRB No. 20, slip op. at 18 (2011) (employer could not "cure" unlawful lockout by submitting its requirements several days after lockout was instituted).

253 Ancor Concepts, 323 NLRB 742, 744 (1997). *See also* Bud Antle, 347 NLRB 87, 89 (2006) ("It is well settled that locked-out employees cannot be permanently replaced.").

254 *See* Hercules Drawn Steel Corp., 352 NLRB 53, 69-70 (2008) (recall of skilled employees did not make lockout unlawful where employer had little or no success in finding temporary replacements).

255 McGwier Co., 204 NLRB 492, 496 (1973) ("[T]here is an obvious disparate treatment of employees in that the Company locked out only those employees who, by striking, had identified themselves as union adherents, while continuing to operate with those employees who had not joined the strike and then later with replacements."); Allen Storage & Moving Co, 342 NLRB 501, 501 (2004) ("Thus, the Respondent, without explanation or justification, allowed Steven Jennings, the only unit employee who had not participated in the strike, to continue work-

ing during both periods of the lockouts, while it barred each former striker from work. Such disparate treatment of former strikers is, as the judge found, evidence of discriminatory motive in the circumstances of this case.").

256 *See* 29 U.S.C §2103(2).

257 International Paper Co., 319 NLRB 1253, 1274-1275 (1995).

258 International Paper Co. v. NLRB, 115 F.3d 1045, 1048-1053 (D.C. Cir. 1997).

259 *See* Alden Leeds, 357 NLRB No. 20, slip op. at 18 (2011); Movers & Warehousemen's Ass'n., 224 NLRB 356, 357 (1976).

260 National Extrusion & Manufacturing Co., 357 NLRB No. 8, slip op. at 5 fn.13 (2011) ("[T]he Respondent's cancellation of employees' health insurance coverage without giving the Union notice and a meaningful opportunity to bargain would have violated Sec. 8(a) (5) and (1) even if the lockout had been lawful."). **Note:** If the lockout is unlawful, a decision to discontinue health benefits violates the NLRA even if the employer offers to bargain. *Id.*

261 *See* Clemson Bros., 290 NLRB 944, 945 (1988) (lockout unlawful because employer refused to furnish union with records verifying its claim that it was unable to pay higher wages); Globe Business Furniture, 290 NLRB 841, fn.2 (1989) (lockout unlawful because, during bargaining, employer refused to provide union with insurance costs and experience data needed to evaluate proposals).

# Index

## Other Books by Robert M. Schwartz

### The Legal Rights of Union Stewards

Topics include stewards' immunity, right to information, Weingarten rights, mid-term bargaining, and duty of fair representation. Over 700,000 copies in print.

### The FMLA Handbook: A Union Guide to the Family and Medical Leave Act

Topics include eligibility, leave rights, notice requirements, grievances, and lawsuits. Over 175,000 copies in print.

### How To Win Past Practice Grievances

Topics include proving a practice, clarifying practices, freestanding practices, and conflicting practices.

### Just Cause: A Union Guide to Winning Discipline Cases

Topics include fair notice, due process, substantial evidence, equal treatment, progressive discipline, and mitigating and extenuating circumstances.

# WORK RIGHTS PRESS
## ORDER FORM

**Please send me:**

_____ copies of *No Contract, No Peace* by Robert M. Schwartz. $20.

_____ copies of *Just Cause: A Union Guide to Winning Disciplinary Cases* by Robert M. Schwartz. $20.

_____ copies of *The Legal Rights of Union Stewards* (4th ed.) by Robert M. Schwartz. $20.

_____ copies of *The FMLA Handbook: A Union Guide to the Family and Medical Leave Act* (4th ed.) by Robert M. Schwartz. $20.

_____ copies of *How to Win Past Practice Grievances* (2nd ed.) by Robert M. Schwartz. $13.

**Shipping and handling:** $4 for first book; $2 for each additional book, maximum $16 for up to 24 books.

For union bulk rates call 800-576-4552 or email workrightspress@igc.org.

I enclose: $_____

_____

*name*

_____

*address*

_____

Fill in and mail with check or money order to Work Rights Press, Box 391066, Cambridge, MA 02139.